THE BASSET HOUND

Bobbye Land

The Basset Hound

Project Team
Editor: Heather Russell-Revesz
Copy Editor: Joann Woy
Indexer: Joann Woy
Design: Stephanie Krautheim
Series Design: Stephanie Krautheim and Mada Design
Series Originator: Dominique De Vito

T.F.H. Publications
President/CEO: Glen S. Axelrod
Executive Vice President: Mark E. Johnson
Publisher: Christopher T. Reggio
Production Manager: Kathy Bontz

T.F.H. Publications, Inc.
One TFH Plaza
Third and Union Avenues
Neptune City, NJ 07753

ISBN 978-0-7938-3626-0

Printed and bound in China
10 11 12 13 14   5 7 9 8 6 4

Library of Congress Cataloging-in-Publication Data
Land, Bobbye.
The basset hound / Bobbye Land.
p. cm.
  Includes index.
ISBN 0-7938-3642-5 (alk. paper)
1. Basset hound. I. Title.
SF429.B2L36 2005
636.753'6—dc22
                    2005022134

This book has been published with the intent to provide accurate and authoritative information in regard to the subject matter within. While every reasonable precaution has been taken in preparation of this book, the author and publisher expressly disclaim responsibility for any errors, omissions, or adverse effects arising from the use or application of the information contained herein. The techniques and suggestions are used at the reader's discretion and are not to be considered a substitute for veterinary care. If you suspect a medical problem consult your veterinarian.

The Leader In Responsible Animal Care For Over 50 Years!®
www.tfh.com

TABLE OF CONTENTS

Chapter 1
HISTORY OF THE BASSET HOUND 5
Viva la Basset—The Breed in France • The Basset in England • The Basset in
America • Star Turns—Famous Basset Hounds

Chapter 2
CHARACTERISTICS OF THE BASSET HOUND 17
A Standard for Excellence • Is the Basset Hound Right for You? • Take the Basset Quiz

Chapter 3
PREPARING FOR YOUR BASSET HOUND 31
Before You Take the Plunge • Where to Find the Basset of Your Dreams • Bringing
Home Basset • How to Travel with Your Basset • When You Can't Take Your
Basset With You

Chapter 4
FEEDING YOUR BASSET HOUND 59
Commercial Food • Bones and Raw Foods (BARF) Diet • Homecooked Diet •
Feeding Schedules • Nutrition for the Senior Basset • The Healthy, Well-Fed
Basset • The Overweight Basset • Mind Your Manners

Chapter 5
GROOMING YOUR BASSET HOUND 81
Commercial Food • Bones and Raw Foods (BARF) Diet • Homecooked Diet •
Feeding Schedules • Nutrition for the Senior Basset • The Healthy, Well-Fed
Basset • The Overweight Basset • Mind Your Manners

Chapter 6
TRAINING AND BEHAVIOR OF YOUR BASSET HOUND 95
Socialization: Why Is it Important? • The Basics: Understanding and Setting Rules
• Types of Training • Housetraining and Crate Training • Leash Training • Basic
Commands • Problem Behaviors

Chapter 7
ADVANCED TRAINING AND ACTIVITIES WITH YOUR
BASSET HOUND 131
Your Dog: Your Partner, Your Friend • Organized Activities for Your Basset • Fun
and Games

Chapter 8
HEALTH OF YOUR BASSET HOUND 151
Choosing a Veterinarian • Puppy's First Vet Trip • Yearly Exams for Your Basset •
Vaccinations • Problems Specific to the Basset Hound • Internal and External
Parasites • Complementary and Alternative Veterinary Medicine (CAVM) • Safety
and First Aid • The Aging Basset • Saying Goodbye

Resources 199

Index 201

HISTORY
of the Basset Hound

he Basset Hound is a breed developed centuries ago in France. The name "Basset" comes from *bas*, the French word for low. Bassets are scent hounds, and were developed to stand low to the ground, in order to hunt game such as rabbits, fox, squirrels, and pheasant in heavy ground cover.

VIVA LA BASSET— THE BREED IN FRANCE

The first mention of the word "Basset" as applied to a breed of dog appears to have been in an early French text on hunting, *La Venerie de Jaques du Fouilloux*, written circa 1585. This book is illustrated with what is considered the first drawing of a Basset—a woodcut showing a sportsman going out in "his *charette de chasse* accompanied by his badger dogs."

The friars of the French Abbey of St. Hubert are believed to have been instrumental in breeding a lower set (shorter-legged), slower-moving hound from various other strains of French hounds, to produce a dog who could more easily be followed on foot. Since hunting was a classic sport in medieval France, it is not surprising that many of these thoroughly efficient, smaller hounds found their way into the kennels of the aristocracy. During the French Revolution, the breed suffered from the changing lifestyle of the aristocracy, but luckily the breed was not lost. Elzear Blaze, in his 1850 sporting book *Le Chasseur*, mentions these hunting hounds. About the same time, in his book *Chiens de Chasse*, M. Robert wrote: "The Basset will hunt all animals, even boar and wolf, but he is especially excellent for the *chasse a tir* (shooting with the aid of hounds) of rabbits and hares."

Two Types of Bassets

By the mid-19th century, the two largest breeders of Bassets in France were producing dogs of slightly different type, especially in head and eye. The two types were identified by the names of their respective breeders: Lane and Le Couteulx. Lane's hounds had broader skulls, shorter ears, and rounder, more prominent eyes. Their markings were generally lemon and white or gray and white, and their front legs had a tendency to knuckle over.

Count Le Couteulx, on the other hand, produced two different types of hounds. One was a larger, heavier-boned, low-to-the-ground hound with a harsher coat that was either red and white or a heavily marked tricolor. The other type was much lighter in build, with a short, fine coat of less well-marked colors, either tricolor or very pale red and white. The Le Couteulx hounds had narrower heads with a more domed skull; a softer, more sunken eye with prominent jaw; and a down-faced look that created a facial expression that the fancy seemed to prefer over the plainer Lane hound.

THE BASSET IN ENGLAND

In 1866, Lord Galway imported a pair of French Bassets of the Le Couteulx type to England. The following year, a mating of these two produced a litter of five pups, but since no public exposure of them occurred, no interest in the breed was stirred. All that changed in 1874, when Sir Everett Millais imported from France a hound named Model. It was from that point on that real activity with the breed began in England. Although Lord Galway was the first to bring the Basset to England, Millais, through the next few years, gained the public exposure and the interest in the breed that Galway had failed to realize. For his support of the breed and continued dedication to a breeding program within his own kennel, as well as cooperation with breeding programs established by Lord Onslow and George Krehl, Sir Everett Millais will forever be considered the "father of the Basset" in England.

Although he was not a showman, and had no prior interest in exhibiting his hounds, Millais entered a Basset in an English dog show in 1875. Apparently, he was bitten by the dog show fever, for five years later he helped make up a large entry for the Wolverhampton show, and there a great deal of public attention was drawn to the breed. Unfortunately, later that year, Millais developed health problems, and he left England for Australia, which ended his breeding career at the time. During the last few years, Millais had made the acquaintance of another Basset fancier,

Lord Onslow. Onslow had imported a bitch and a dog ten years earlier. At the time he met Millais, he wanted to make a more serious effort at establishing the breed in England, so he and Millais interbred the dogs from their packs. When Millais left for Australia, Onslow disbanded his own pack, sending some of his better stock to fellow fancier George Krehl, who continued where Millais and Onslow had left off with their breeding program. Because he had imported new Basset Hounds from France, he could carry on a breeding program on a somewhat wider scale than had been available to Millais and Onslow.

Bringing Uniformity to the Breed

It was a challenge to Krehl to bring more uniformity to the breed. These early Bassets were indeed far from uniform at that time, which is not surprising considering Count le Couteulx's early attempts to develop an entirely new strain. However, using careful breeding practices, Krehl was finally able to consistently perpetuate

The Basset Hound is a breed developed centuries ago in France.

The Bard on Bassets

Even Shakespeare was impressed with the Basset Hound, describing them with this poetic image: "Ears which sweep away the morning dew." Certainly an apt description! But, do you know the original reason for those long ears? The Basset was bred to hunt small game. Those long ears were developed to stir up and hold the scent long enough for their strong nose to inhale. The folds of skin under the chin (the dewlap) aren't there by accident, either. They also help trap and hold the scent, as do the wrinkles about the head and face. Their large feet make them steady, and their heavy bones make them sturdy. They may be more of an "ambler" than some other hunting breeds, but for most hunters on foot, their speed, or rather lack of it, is appreciated because it allows the hunter to closely follow on foot. Every inch of the Basset is a cleverly designed canine machine, developed to be a stable companion, whether in the field, by the hearth, or in the show ring.

the type of one of his favorite original Bassets, Fino de Paris (litter brother to Model). The final touch to the creation of this "perfect hound" came when Krehl imported dogs from the Lane kennels in France, which he then bred to the products of his breeding program, which had been based mainly on dogs from the le Couteulx kennel.

In 1884, Millais returned from Australia and was pleased to find that some of his original kennel stock were still not only alive but available for breeding. He immediately planned an inbreeding (grandfather to granddaughter) that produced what he described as "perfectly satisfactory" puppies. He had "three beautiful pups from this intercourse—namely, Kini, Lady Dollie, and Lady Daisy, all true Bassets and tricolors."

It was that year that the Basset Hound Club was formed in England. Charter members were those who had remained so dedicated to the breed throughout its formative years: Count le Couteulx de Canteleu, the man who was so instrumental in preserving the breed in France; Lords Onslow and Galway, two early importers and breeders of Bassets in England; and Everett Millais and George Krehl.

Soon they were joined by many others, including H.R.H. Princess Alexandra (wife of Edward, Prince of Wales, later Queen Alexandra, wife of King Edward VII) and Mrs. Ellis of Brettenham Park, Billesden. Obviously, it certainly helped stoke interest in the breed when Queen Alexandra kept Basset Hounds in the royal kennels for the first time. She maintained a somewhat large breeding kennel, breeding not only smooth- and rough-coated Bassets, but also Clumber Spaniels. Her kennel name was Sandringham—after the family's favorite summer home—where the dogs were actually kept. Practically all of our present day Bassets are related in one way or the other to Princess Alexandra's dogs, some of whom have been depicted beautifully by the famous animal painter, Arthur Wardle.

Approximately 12 years after the first Bassets were imported to England from France, 120 Basset were entered at the Dachshund and Basset Show at the Aquarium in London. Fittingly, the judge for Bassets for the day was Everett Millais.

Sad at seeing the loss of bone and substance and the lack of intelligence in current Bassets, Millais himself began a crossbreeding program to bring those qualities back. He also wanted to bring back the intelligence that owners now were claiming was lacking. Crossbreeding was nothing new to Millais, because he had earlier crossbred Beagles into his Basset Hound kennel. This time, Millais chose the Bloodhound for his crossbreeding. In doing so, he did not "improve" the Basset as it had been imported from France years earlier—he created a new breed entirely. He created today's Basset Hound.

Although that first crossbred litter tragically lost not only the dam but five of the twelve puppies, the surviving puppies went on to be the backbone of what would become the Basset Hound as we recognize it today.

Did You Know?

Some historians believe George Washington owned Basset Hounds given to him by Lafayette after the American Revolution.

THE BASSET IN AMERICA

Although the Basset came to the US in colonial times, the breed did not come into its own in this country until early in the 20th century. Recognized by the American Kennel Club (AKC) in 1885, it was not until the early 1900s, when several easterners imported dogs from leading kennels in England, that the development of the heavier, bigger-boned American-type Bassets began.

It took a few years for the breed to gain in popularity. On February 28, 1928, *Time* magazine featured a Basset Hound on the front cover of the magazine. The accompanying cover story was a write-up of the 52nd annual Westminster Kennel Club dog show at Madison Square Garden, written as if it were attended and observed by a Basset Hound puppy. Since then, the Basset has secured his place in the hearts of many, and is one of the 25 most popular breeds in the United States.

The first annual meeting of the Basset Hound Club of America (BHCA) took place in Michigan, in 1935. The first Basset Hound field trial was held in that year, also in Michigan. And, in 1937, the first AKC licensed field trial for Bassets took place with five entered. Hillcrest Peggy, owned by Emil and Effie Seitz, was the winner. Less than a year later, she became the first Basset Hound field champion. Lulu's Red, owned by Walter and Marge Brandt, became the first Basset to receive a Companion Dog obedience title, in 1947.

Bassets became popular show dogs, although it was 15 years

Basset Hounds have never forgotten their humble beginnings as part of a hunter's pack.

Breed Clubs

The American Kennel Club (AKC), founded in 1884, is the most influential dog club in the United States. The AKC is a "club of clubs," meaning that its members are other kennel clubs, not individual people. The AKC registers purebred dogs, supervises dog shows, and is concerned with all dog-related matters, including public education and legislation. It collects and publishes the official standards for all of its recognized breeds.

The United Kingdom version of the AKC is called the Kennel Club. However, the Kennel Club's members are individual persons. The membership of the Kennel Club is restricted to a maximum of 1,500 UK members, in addition to 50 overseas members and a small number of honorary life members. The Kennel Club promotes responsible dog ownership and works on important issues like canine health and welfare.

after the BHCA was formed that the first Basset stood on the Best in Show podium at an all-breed conformation show. That dog was Ch. Anthony of St. Hubert, owned by Mark Washbond. With their Bloodhound genes, it would seem that tracking would be a snap for the Basset, but most people did not attempt to title their dogs in tracking until years later. In fact, the first Basset to attain a Tracking Dog title was Ludwig von B., owned by Stephen and Anna Sandberg, in 1961. In 1964, a new conformation standard was approved by the AKC and the BHCA—the standard that is still accepted by both and adhered to by breeders to this day.

Basset Hounds have never forgotten their humble beginning as part of a hunter's pack. Their nose and steadfast determination make them favorites among serious hunters—especially rabbit hunters. In later years, field titles were granted to Basset Hounds at AKC field tests. Kazoo's Moses the Great, owned by Jim and Pat Dohr, was the first Basset to win a Dual Championship (show champion and field champion). In 1972, the Grand Field Champion title for Bassets was established. Hamlin's Dolly, owned by Ewing Carhart; McWilliams' Dixie Belle, owned by Ken McWilliams; and Van's Fantasy, owned by Tom Pettit, were the first winners of this new title.

Fédération Cynologique Internationale

While many people have only heard of the American Kennel Club, Kennel Club, and perhaps some other national kennel clubs, an international organization actually exists. The Fédération Cynologique Internationale is the World Canine Organization, which includes 80 members and contract partners (one member per country), each of which issues its own pedigrees and trains its own judges. The founding nations were Germany, Austria, Belgium, France, and the Netherlands. It was first formed in 1911, but later disappeared during World War I. The organization was reconstituted in 1921. Currently, neither the United States nor Canada is a member.

The FCI ensures that its pedigrees and judges are recognized by all FCI members. Every member country conducts international shows as well as working trials; results are sent to the FCI office, where they are input into computers. When a dog has been awarded a certain number of awards, he can receive the title of International Beauty or Working Champion. These titles are confirmed by the FCI.

The FCI recognizes 331 dog breeds, and each of them is the "property" of a specific country, ideally the one in which the breed developed. The owner countries of the breeds write the standard of these breeds in cooperation with the Standards and Scientific Commissions of the FCI, and the translation and updating are carried out by the FCI.

In addition, via the national canine organization and the FCI, every breeder can ask for international protection of his or her kennel name.

FAMOUS BASSET HOUNDS

It was bound to happen that Basset Hounds would catch the eye of people everywhere who saw in the loveable Basset a face the public would trust and adore. In alphabetical order, the following Bassets became famous through TV and/or advertising:

- Cleo the Basset Hound (played by Bernadette the dog) was seen weekly on the sitcom *The People's Choice* (NBC, 1955–1958). Cleopatra ("Cleo") observed and commented on the weekly predicaments of her master Socrates "Sock" Miller (Jackie Cooper), a Bureau of Fish and Wildlife ornithologist who was elected city councilman of Barkerville, a California housing development. Cleo never spoke, but her wise-cracking thoughts could be heard loud and clear (voiced by Mary Jane Croft). In 1958, Cleo was a winner of a PATSY (Picture Animals

Top Star of the Year) Award. Cleo also appeared in *Little Golden Book #287, Cleo* (Simon & Schuster, 1957), written by Irwin Shapiro, with photos by Durward B. Graybill.

- Dog, a Basset Hound, was seen on many episodes of the TV police drama *Columbo* (NBC, 1971–1977; ABC, 1989–1991). On TV, Dog was owned by Lt. Columbo (played by Peter Falk), who seemed as bumblingly incompetent as Bassets sometimes appear to those unfamiliar with the breed. Columbo and Dog also were proof that sometimes owners and their dogs begin to look alike. Dog also appeared in each of the Columbo movies. In real life, Dog was known as Henry. Henry was an old hat at the TV scene, having appeared on the medical drama *Emergency* (NBC, 1972–1977) in the role of the mascot for the Los Angeles County Squad 51 firehouse, a dog who just sat about and yawned. Quite a stretch for a Basset—what an actor!

- On the TV show *The Dukes of Hazzard* (CBS, 1979–1985), Basset Hound Flash was owned by Sheriff Rosco P. Coltrane (who referred to Flash lovingly as "Velvet Ears"). Rosco proclaimed her to be a "well trained attack dog," but few ever saw Flash do much except eat, sleep, and bark at the wrong people. The part of Flash was played by several dogs, including a life-sized stuffed replica that was used as a stunt-dog. The primary dog for most scenes was a Basset named Sandy, who was adopted from a local animal shelter.

- During the 1950s, a Basset named Morgan was used on several comedy sketches on the *Garry Moore Show*. Morgan was owned by TV producer Dick Gordon. Morgan became so popular that, in 1973, a New York city department store

Bassets have been featured in media and advertising for years—probably because of their loveable faces.

Christmas catalogue featured a "Huggable Morgan"—a stuffed Basset made of plush rayon with a squeaker in its nose.

- Fans of the sitcom *Coach* (ABC, 1989–1997) are familiar with Luther Van Dam's beloved Basset Hound, Quincy. Quincy's "tricks" included lying in one place and doing nothing, and riding in a little red wagon because he was too lazy to walk. (Again, what a stretch of acting ability for a Basset.) A dog named Isaac played the part of Quincy until he died. Quincy was then written out of the show via a funeral episode that featured the ceremony Luther planned when he lost his best friend. At the end of the service, Luther's friends presented him with another puppy. Isaac was a veteran performer who appeared in a recurring role on NBC's daytime soap opera *Santa Barbara* as well as in a series of Purina Dog Food commercials.

- Sherlock. Locked in a ratings war with Ed Sullivan, comedian Steve Allen had a brainstorm that paid off well. He hired the talents of a young and upcoming singer, Elvis Presley, to dress

Basset Tidbits

- In trailing ability, the accuracy of a Basset's nose makes him second only to the Bloodhound.
- The foremost use of the Basset in the US is hunting rabbits.
- The Basset's leg bones are the heaviest of any breed of any size.
- The word "basset" in French, the Basset Hound's country of origin, means "low slung."
- Because the Basset was originally bred to hunt in packs, they have retained a leisurely attitude towards other canines, which make them wonderful additions to multi-dog households.

in white tie and tails and sing "Hound Dog" to Basset Hound Sherlock, who wore a top hat. Elvis and RCA continued to use Sherlock for publicity throughout the 1950s.

- A Basset named Jason was featured in a 1988 Hush Puppies shoe ad for "Ventilated Hush Puppies." Remember the scene Marilyn Monroe made a classic, when she stood on an air grate with her skirt whooshing up in *The Seven Year Itch*? In the Hush Puppy ad, a whoosh of air from the subway below sent Jason's ears flying upward.

Although many changes have been made to the breed throughout the years, the Basset we see today would likely bring a contented smile to the faces of those who first created the breed so many decades ago, and to those who sought through the years to protect and perfect it. The Basset Hound continues to be a happy hunter and devoted friend to this day.

CHARACTERISTICS
of the Basset Hound

t only takes one look at a Basset Hound to know that he was bred to be a hunter. Low to the ground and sturdily built, Bassets give the illusion of being a much smaller dog than they in fact are. (Try to pick up a Basset Hound, and you'll see what I mean—he doesn't really qualify as a lap dog.) It's been said that a Basset is a Bloodhound (a great grandfather of the breed) body set on Dachshund legs—a fairly apt description. Watching a Basset moving along, you might liken him to a cartoon character or a clumsy clown. However, the Basset is in truth a very agile and surefooted dog; while he may never be considered truly graceful due to the nature of his design, his movement is poetry in motion to a true Basset fancier.

A STANDARD FOR EXCELLENCE

The breed standard tells you the desired physical makeup and temperament of Basset Hounds. So, let's go point by point through the breed standard and see what kind of dog it describes. After all, how else will you know the perfect Basset when you see it?

Head

We'll start with the head, since that's usually the first part of a dog that you notice. The Basset head is definitely unique. Whereas other breeds and mixed breeds may be described as having "sort of a Basset head," the ideal Basset resembles nothing more than himself. The skull is rounded, never flat, with a deep muzzle. The skin is loose on the face and heavily wrinkled over the brow when the dog's head is lowered to sniff the trail. The loose skin is so important to the breed's distinction that it is mentioned as a fault in the standard for any Basset to have smooth, tight skin on the head.

The combination of the pendulous ears (their length is so important that the standard spells out that they should fold well over the end of the nose when extended and be velvety in texture, with the ends curling slightly inward), deep facial wrinkles, and pendulous lips is for a reason other than appearance—together, they gather scents towards the nose, allowing the Basset to adequately

What Is a Standard?

A standard is a written description providing a mental picture of the ideal dog in any pure breed approved first by the breed's parent club and then by the national kennel club. It describes the characteristics that distinguish one breed from another.

The present AKC standard for Basset Hounds was submitted by the Basset Hound Club of America and accepted by the American Kennel Club in early 1964. The present standard for Basset Hounds in Great Britain was accepted by their Kennel Club in March 1994.

do his job. His job, as a seeker of smells, is such an important part of who he is that even his nostrils are mentioned in the standard: They are required to be large and wide-open, set on a muzzle that is deep and heavy.

The occiput (back part of the head or skull) is mentioned several times in the breed standard. First as a measuring point: "The length of the head from occiput to muzzle is greater than the width at the brow," then described in detail "…the skull is well domed, showing a pronounced occipital protuberance."

Teeth

The teeth are important in any breed, but the standard states firmly that a Basset's should be large, sound, regular, and in either a scissors or even bite. The head is set on a neck that is powerful and not only of proper length, but well arched.

Eyes

No Basset head can be complete without classic Basset eyes: soft, sad, dark (light eyes are permissible with some coat colors, but extremely light eyes are considered incorrect no matter the coat color), and slightly sunken, with a prominent but not overdone haw (the red portion inside the eyelids). People who own Bassets are quick to say that although the eyes appear sad at first glance, they often show a mischievous twinkle in their depths.

Body

The next thing you notice about Bassets is their unusual body shape. Unlike most breeds, a Basset's sternum (chest) sticks out in front of his legs. (Some Basset owners laughingly refer to it as a Dolly Parton chest.) The shoulders and elbows are set tight against the chest, and although the front legs are allowed to have a bow, they should never knuckle over (a disqualification), and the elbows should never push away from the body. The ribs should be well sprung, without making the dog appear barrel chested. This allows room for the good-sized heart and lungs necessary for a working dog.

The Basset is a low-slung dog, with the distance from the deepest point of the chest to the ground never being more than one-third the total height at the withers. His topline should be straight and level, free from any tendency towards sagging (considered a fault in the breed).

The Basset Hound's eyes are famously soft, sad, and dark.

Legs and Feet

A Basset's legs should be of dense, heavy bone. The feet should be well rounded and with both feet inclined equally a trifle outward, which balances the width of the shoulders. The feet should be strong and sturdy. The toes should not be splayed nor pinched together, and they should create a nicely rounded outline edge instead of a point. The feet are so important that even a Basset's paws are described in their ideal in the breed standard. They should be massive and heavy, with tough pads.

Unlike most breeds, a Basset's chest sticks out in front of his legs.

A Basset is just as recognizable from the rear as from the front. With full and well-rounded hindquarters that stand firm with no sign of crouching, the rear legs have a nicely angled stifle, with hocks that are parallel. The hind feet always point straight ahead and should never point either in or out.

Tail

A Basset carries his undocked tail gaily and proudly, slightly curving over his back. The hair on the underside of the tail is coarse, never long nor curly.

Coat

The Basset's coat is short, hard, and dense (with a loose, elastic skin), which makes him truly "weather resistant" and able to carry on with his job no matter the weather. A long coat (especially one with waves or curls) is a disqualification. The color and pattern is typical of other hound breeds: tricolor (black, red, and white), red and white, or lemon and white are preferred. Blue—actually a shade of gray—is accepted within the standard, but is not preferred by breeders because it is

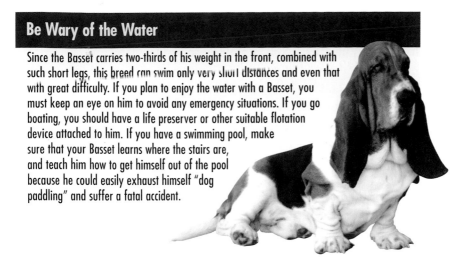

believed to be associated with some genetic problems.

Height and Weight

Bassets should be no more than 14 inches (35.5 cm) at the shoulder, but because of the heavy bones and muscles, they can weigh between 40 and 80 pounds (18 and 36 kg). Definitely not small lap dogs, although they do enjoy being that close to their humans. They are much longer than tall, a conformation that can cause back problems if the dog is not managed and maintained properly, with great care taken for his safety.

Movement

Although Basset Hounds are big dogs, they move with a gracefulness that belies their size. They should never lumber, but move fluidly, in a smooth, powerful, and effortless manner. Unlike some breeds that are shown during dog shows with their heads held high in the air, a Basset's true movement holds his nose low to the ground, always searching for that elusive scent. Perfect coordination should be present between the front and rear legs, and they should move in a straight and true line, with the hind feet following directly behind the front feet. They should never move with a stiff gait, nor should their front legs paddle, weave, or overlap. The elbows should remain close to the body as they trot.

Temperament

The Basset's temperament should be mild, never sharp or timid.

He is a dog not only capable of great endurance in the field, but is extreme in his devotion to you as well. The typical Basset is eager to please, quick to learn, and willing to obey.

IS THE BASSET HOUND RIGHT FOR YOU?

The Basset Hound is a suitable dog for almost any situation, as long as he is treated with love and respect and given adequate care for his particular needs. The Basset's history makes him adaptable to myriad situations including work (as a tracking or field companion), exhibition (obedience, agility, conformation, and the like), or simply being a pet for an owner of almost any age. Usually a docile and calm animal, the Basset is definitely a "people dog" and should never be considered by anyone who is not going to be able to enjoy a lot of quality time with his or her dog.

Because of their heavy bones and muscles, Bassets can weigh quite a bit.

Rare Bassets

Don't be lured into purchasing a Basset Hound that does not fit the breed standard simply because he is advertised as "rare." Once in a while, you'll see someone advertise a "blue" Basset, sometimes not only for sale, but with an exaggerated price tag. "Blue" (actually blue-gray) is not an accepted hound color, therefore it is not desirable for Bassets. Being "unusual" or "rare" does not make a dog worth more; in fact, he should come with a marked-down price, as in the case of this color, which has been linked with hair loss and a poor, thin coat.

A blue-eyed Basset is not acceptable for conformation exhibition or breeding according to the BHCA breed standard, which calls for brown eyes. And, although a dog who has a "blue" coat or eyes will be as special as a pet as any other Basset, they should not be considered "desirable" and certainly never considered as part of a breeding program. Remember, "rare" doesn't always mean desirable, and in this case, it certainly doesn't deserve a higher price.

City or Country Dog?

Although a large dog, most Bassets are easily adaptable to apartment living, as long as they are given adequate walks on a leash, although most would prefer a nice sized yard or enclosed field for romping.

Exercise Needs

Bassets need only moderate exercise; however, the couch potato Basset will be prone to pack on extra pounds that can be very detrimental to his health, given his long, low profile. It is advised that any Basset be given regular exercise either in a confined, fenced area or on a leash. Short daily walks that are strictly for toilet purposes are not enough exercise to keep extra pounds from showing up on the Basset's body.

Attention

Although a Basset Hound is adaptable to almost any type of living arrangements (provided that he has adequate room for exercise), he will be happiest in a home where someone is home with him during the day, and preferably in a place that has a secure fenced area where he can occasionally romp and play on his own. The average Basset Hound is a versatile dog who will likely be just as much at home in the field on hunting trips as he is in your

Bassets can be at home in the city, suburbs, or country.

backyard fetching tennis balls for the neighborhood kids.

Left alone for long periods of time, a Basset (like any dog) will become bored and can get into trouble. Their voice is definitely part of their character, and many learn to love the sound of their own voice bouncing around empty rooms or yards. This can definitely cause a problem for the owner with nearby neighbors.

Other Pets

Because Bassets were bred to hunt in packs, they are excellent additions to any multi-pet household, as long as the initial introductions are handled well.

Training

The Basset is a sturdy, loyal pet who is easy to train (as long as training sessions are kept interesting). He can be quite stubborn at times, so if you're not willing to be patient and creative during training sessions, keep looking for your perfect pet—it won't be a Basset.

The Dreaded Drool

Although the Basset makes a wonderful companion, he is not the perfect dog for everyone. If you are an exemplary housekeeper who finds dog hair and slobber offensive, it's best to look for another breed. Bassets shed no more than any other breed, and less than some, but their slobber and drool is usually very effusive and can be quite difficult to get used to. The primary reason for owners turning a Basset in to a rescue network is the amount of drool they can create and "share."

Grooming Needs

Although Bassets are considered "wash and wear" dogs, they are prone to the body odor that is familiar to most hound breeds. People who live with a lot of hounds don't notice the smell after a while, but newcomers find it hard to miss. Many times, the odor associated with a Basset won't stem from body odor at all, but come from his ears. Because the ears are low and pendulous, you may find them prone to infections and other medical maladies from lack of air circulation. (See Chapter 5 for more on ear care for your Basset.)

Outdoor Supervision

If you can't keep him confined or extremely well supervised every moment he is out of doors, it's best to choose a different breed. Any Basset that is allowed to get his feet under him as he chases a smell will be a lost Basset in minutes. Because of their ability to cover large areas of ground in a short amount of time, a lost Basset may remain so even with the most diligent of searches. Since this is a Hound breed, bred to trail prey through thick underbrush, their sense of smell combined with an inquisitive nature makes it impossible for them to be allowed out into the world on their own without supervision and makes it necessary for them to be kept controlled on a leash.

Children

The Basset's intelligence and adept clumsiness, paired with his loyalty and trustworthiness, make this breed one of the most

Do Your Research

When researching breeds, make sure that you learn the good with the bad. There is no perfect breed. They all have problems: health, temperament, daily-care needs, or even a mixture of all three. Discuss with each family member what he or she will expect from this new family addition and decide definitely whether this particular breed will truly fit all your needs and expectations. After the purchase is made, it is too late for such considerations.

Children should be taught how to interact with dogs before you consider adopting one.

desired for a family pet. However, it's impossible to answer the question, "Are Bassets good with children?" without first answering the question, "Is this child good with dogs?" Children should be taught how to interact with animals, especially dogs, long before you consider adopting a dog as a pet. Children and dogs left alone together with no supervision are an accident waiting to happen. Dog bites very seldom occur when a parent or guardian is supervising their interaction.

No dog should be expected to continually take abuse at the hands of any human, no matter how small those hands. Children should be advised of the dangers of teasing or provoking any dog, and when problems occur, common sense should be exhibited before you jump to a conclusion that can have disastrous results for an innocent dog. Problems between dogs and children are usually easily preventable with combination of responsible dog training and responsible parenting.

TAKE THE BASSET QUIZ

Have you decided if you are indeed a Basset Hound person? Let's see how you honestly answer the following questions:

- Are you and your entire family committed to spending the next 8 to 12 years providing health care, food, grooming, training, and love for a family pet?
- Do you have the time available to take your dog for walks and to the vet? To bathe and groom your Basset as often as necessary?
- Will you be willing to teach your children to respect your dog's space, and teach them to handle and treat the dog properly? Will your children follow the "house rules" you've set for the pet?
- Are events in your future coming that could provide life-altering changes? Things such as having a baby, caring for elderly parents, a divorce or job change, financial insecurity, that might alter your ability to care for a pet? If these things came up unexpectedly, would taking care of your Basset still be a top priority?
- Is your personality conducive to responsible dog ownership? Are you patient? Flexible? Loving and nurturing? Are you a neat freak who wants everything in its place both inside and outside your home? Would dog hair or drool on the furniture be considered a major problem?
- Are you physically, financially, and emotionally able to care for a dog on a day-to-day basis?
- Is your home environment prepared to adequately accommodate a Basset? Or are you willing to make the investment of time and money necessary to ensure that it is? Is your yard, or a portion of it, securely fenced?
- Will you or another family member be home during the day, at least for a while, to attend to your new pet's needs?
- Do you have the time and inclination to train a new puppy? If the answer is "no," would you consider adopting an older dog as a companion, instead of a puppy?
- Do you enjoy meeting new people? It's a given that taking a

Basset Tidbit

The Basset has been lovingly described as having the head and bone of a Bloodhound, coloring of a Foxhound, and legs of a Dachshund.

Basset Pros and Cons

If you want a dog who displays the following characteristics, then a Basset Hound may indeed be the right dog for you:

• Is a mild-mannered, gentle, calm member of the family;

• Needs only moderate exercise;

• Is sociable with not only humans but other animals as well;

• Is adaptable to almost any situation, job, or performance you ask of him;

• Has a distinctive look, with a face that makes everyone smile.

However, if you are not certain you can deal with the following you should perhaps check out a different breed:

• Stubbornness and a need for creative training;

• Running away (oblivious to your calls) when an interesting scent catches his nose;

• Howling;

• Drooling and slobbering;

• Heavy shedding;

• A distinctive "houndy" odor;

• Gassiness or flatulence;

• Being prone to injury because of his distinct build (long and low).

walk with your Basset Hound will bring attention to both you and your pet, and passers-by will inevitably stop you to chat about the "Basset they had as a child" or how they "always enjoyed hunting trips with their dad and the family Basset Hound when they were growing up."

• And, last but most important, are you ready to share your home with an ebullient clown who will find or create humor in any situation—one who will love you with an astounding devotion, no matter whether you deserve it or not, and fill a hole in your life that you weren't aware was even there?

If you answered yes to these questions, then you're undoubtedly going to make an excellent "Basset Hound person."

Remember, no breed has a single list of characteristics that are true for every single dog. Find your dog from a source you can trust and be honest with them about everything you expect from your dog. Temperaments vary between littermates, as well as within bloodlines. A concerned breeder will do her best to find the dog who best fits your family's lifestyle, your schedule, your home type (apartment, farm, house, etc.), your performance plans (obedience, agility, hunting, conformation exhibition, etc.), as well as your general expectations. A good breeder wants you to be happy with your dog, so that your dog will be happy with you.

Bassets are adaptable to almost any situation.

PREPARING

for Your Basset Hound

f you've ever purchased a car, you probably did your homework and gathered as much information as possible regarding its safety record, fuel needs, maintenance, and daily operational requirements. Yet, a car is a machine that will stay with you only a few years and will never be considered "part of the family." Doesn't the acquisition of a living, breathing family member deserve at least an equal consideration?

Before you decide to get a dog, you should first discuss it thoroughly with every member of the family—remembering that every opinion must be carefully considered. A dog chosen for the right reasons after careful research quickly becomes a valued family member. On the other hand, if a dog is chosen for the wrong reason, or is the wrong breed of dog he can (through no fault of his own) quickly become a burden. Having a dog—like anything in life—has its pros and cons. For instance, playing ball in the park with your new best friend is fun. Scooping poop on a rainy day is not.

BEFORE YOU TAKE THE PLUNGE

Before brining the new addition into your family, there are a few questions that need to be answered.

Why Do You Want a Dog?

First and most importantly, ask yourself why you want a dog before you jump into making a purchase you might regret. If the answer to this question is:

- *For the children.* Consider that although every child will certainly benefit from growing up with a dog as his best friend, once the newness of the situation has worn off, it will undoubtedly end up being the responsibility of the parents to provide daily care for the dog. You should give the matter a lot more thought before making your final decision.

Cost and Effect

Not only will your new addition likely come with a hefty price tag, but the expenses can easily add up over the year, just in normal food, supplies, and routine medical care. Unless you learn to bathe and groom your dog, you'll also have the expense of hiring a professional groomer to do the job for you. If you do groom your dog, you'll have the initial expense of buying grooming tools. Factor in the possibility for accidents and other associated expenses, and you'll realize that adding a dog to the family can be almost as expensive as adding another human member.

- *For protection.* An alarm system, security fence, or any of a dozen other measures are not only more effective in most situations—they are far less expensive in the long run than adding a canine burglar alarm. Don't expect a Basset to have the temperament of a guardian breed, either. Although Bassets have a healthy, deep, husky bark that might deter a robber, most would happily lead a burglar to the family's hidden treasure chest for a handful of dog treats.

- *To breed puppies and make money.* The breeding of dogs is a responsibility not to be taken lightly. Dogs are living, breathing creatures, and dog breeding requires a significant investment of time, money, labor, knowledge (both academic and practical), and patience to be done responsibly and humanely. Visit a shelter and look at the faces of the homeless dogs before you consider breeding.

- *Because the breed is so cool or just appeared in a movie.* Choosing a breed of dog solely because of its physical appearance, or its popularity due to publicity, is one of the absolute worst reasons. Often, movies and TV shows star rare or unique breeds that are unsuitable for most normal family situations.

- *Because we found one that's free or cheap.* Remember that when you're adopting a dog, you're likely to get what you pay for. A "free" or "cheap" dog may cost you significantly more in veterinarian bills, training costs, and other considerations. Choosing a family member to share your life is definitely not the time to cut corners.

- *We want a companion to live with us and share our home, and we're willing to wait until the right puppy or adult comes along!* Aha! Finally, the correct answer! This should be the only reason to make the decision to purchase a dog. You may have different activities you want to share with your pet, like hunting, conformation showing, or performance events, but your basic request should be to find the dog who will fit in with your family's lifestyle and be considered a part of the family.

Puppy or Adult?

The next decision is whether you want a puppy or an adult dog. There's no doubt that nothing is cuter in the world than a Basset Hound puppy. With their drooping ears and eyes and gleeful waddle, they charm the heart of everyone they meet. But, having your heart charmed and being realistic about what your family needs and wants are two different things.

Remember that a puppy is going to need much the same attention and time spent on him as a human baby. While he won't be a baby for quite as long as a human, he will have special needs for long enough to disrupt almost anyone's schedule. Between having to be watched constantly to keep him out of trouble, being fed four times a day, and taken outside to potty every 3 to 4 hours, a puppy is indeed a weighty responsibility. Add into the mix that a young puppy is going to need all his basic training as well as veterinary checkups every couple of weeks.

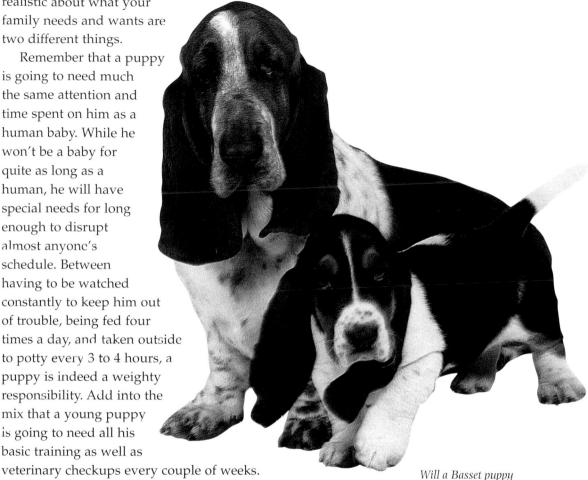

Will a Basset puppy or adult be right for you?

If you decide you're not quite ready for the responsibility and time involved in raising a puppy, you might be a good candidate for adopting a rescued or other preowned adult Basset. Sometimes, older pets fare better around small children than would a young puppy, who might be more rambunctious and harm a child without meaning to. Also, adult Bassets are large enough to romp and play with the kids without worrying quite so much about the kids harming the dog. An older pet is an excellent choice for senior citizens or physically challenged adults who may not have the energy, ability, or desire to keep up with a younger puppy. An older dog has the added advantage of possibly being housetrained already, and even if not, they're more easily put on a schedule than a puppy who seems to have to piddle every 20 minutes.

As for the fear that your new pet won't bond with you as well as a younger puppy would? Forget it! Any dog professional will agree that an older adopted dog appreciates your care and quickly becomes even more devoted—after all, he likely knows what it's like to live in a world without love.

Of course, an older dog may come with pre-existing problems, so it's important to go to a source that tests temperament and is honest about a dog's behavior.

Adult pets can come from many sources—shelters, private parties, classifieds, or breed-rescue groups. Many breeders will offer their retired champions to pet homes, as well as occasionally having older puppies available for one reason or another. In either case, their loss is your gain.

Registering Your Dog

If you received a registration application with your puppy, or registration certificate with an older dog, it will be easy to get him registered in your name with the American Kennel Club or other canine registry. The previous owner should have signed in the appropriate place indicating that they were transferring ownership of the dog to you and dated it accordingly. They should have been present when you signed the papers indicating that you accepted ownership of the dog on said date, and you wish to be recorded as his present owner, residing at the address you include in the proper section. Mailed to the registration office (the address will be plainly printed on the registration papers) with the appropriate fee, you should receive your registration certificate within 4 to 6 weeks, showing you as the recorded owner.

If you were not given or promised registration papers or an application for registration at the time of purchase, it will be very difficult (if not impossible) to trace down your dog's registerability. If you want to exhibit in AKC performance events, and you are certain your dog is a purebred, you can get an Indefinite Listing Privilege (ILP) number that allows you to participate.

In England, the breeder should register the litter with the Kennel Club (assuming the litter is eligible), then provide you with transfer of ownership papers with everything signed and ready for you to send in. When you send in this paperwork, ownership is transferred to you, and the puppy is officially registered.

Whatever you decide—choosing a puppy or an older dog—the key things are to be sure you're ready for the responsibility of owning a dog and to take your time in the search for the perfect dog for your family. The right dog is out there, just waiting for you to find him and let him love you. When you finally look in his eyes, you'll know he was well worth the wait!

When you visit the breeder, check over the pups to make sure they look healthy.

Pet or Show Quality?

After you've decided on a puppy or an adult, you now have to decide what you expect to do with your new pet. Do you want a companion to snuggle with on the couch to watch TV, join you on early morning jogs, or go with your family to the beach or on fishing trips? Do you want to get involved in performance events such as agility, obedience, or tracking? Would you enjoy hunting with your friend? Or perhaps entering competitive hunt tests in which your dog is judged on his instincts and abilities (this is a breed that originated specifically as a hunter's companion)? Maybe you've watched a few dog shows on TV, and you've attended your local kennel club show and decided that showing dogs looks like fun. You must have a firm idea in mind of what you want to do with your Basset when you contact breeders, because "pet or show quality?" will be one of their first questions.

If you decide on a pet-quality dog, don't think that you're getting a puppy of lesser quality, or that your puppy should be bargain-basement priced because he has some flaw. Sometimes, the only differences between a "show puppy" and a "pet puppy" are markings, tail length, or other seemingly frivolous details. Breeders must be very choosy about which dogs they keep to show. Showing dogs is an expensive sport, and only the best should be kept for exhibition and future breeding plans. Breeders invest a lot of knowledge, time, and money to create those cute little bundles, and even the puppies who are somewhat less than perfect for one reason or another still have the potential to give you many years of love and companionship beyond compare.

If you choose a pet puppy, be expected to be given AKC Limited Registration papers. This means that, although your puppy is AKC registered, its offspring could not be registered. If your puppy was

Remember, owning a dog is a long-term commitment.

Pedigrees and Registrations

Even a mixed-breed dog at the shelter could have a written pedigree, if you knew who his parents and grandparents were. A pedigree is simply a "family tree"—it does not denote quality. You and I have a pedigree, but few of us are champions. (Some of us, in fact, may not even be "show quality!")

Being registered simply means that a pedigree for each of the ancestors of your puppy was provided to the American Kennel Club or other registration organization, and each following generation has been declared "purebred" and issued their own personal pedigree. The registration does not denote quality of health, temperament, or appearance by the AKC or any other registration organization.

not good enough for the breeder to keep it to show and possibly breed, they will likely feel that it should not be allowed to reproduce. If a breeder offers you a pet puppy and does not discuss spaying or neutering with you, you might want to check into their references a bit more carefully.

If a breeder has a puppy good enough to be termed "show quality," he or she will expect the dog to be shown. If you are willing to take on the added responsibility of showing a dog (very expensive and time consuming), then by all means, discuss a show prospect. But if not, be honest and tell the breeder that you simply want a good quality pet.

Be wary of breeders who offer "show quality" puppies if they do not themselves show dogs, or if neither parent is a finished champion. Unfortunately, that term is becoming a catch phrase for folks trying to sell puppies. You should ask the breeder who they brought in to evaluate these puppies and what their qualification was for doing so. Most veterinarians, unless they themselves breed and show this specific breed, are not qualified to determine the breed standard quality of a puppy or adult. They can tell you that the dog is healthy, and they can possibly determine if he is likely purebred, but they cannot determine show quality. Only someone who is knowledgeable about the breed, one who consistently and successfully breeds and shows that breed at conformation events, or someone who is licensed to judge that breed is qualified to determine "show quality."

One advantage to purchasing your Basset from a good breeder is that you can meet the mother—one of the best ways to check for temperament.

So, have you decided yet? Are you sure you're ready to share your heart and home with a dog? Once you're certain that a Basset Hound is what you are looking for, you must then be willing to wait until the perfect puppy becomes available. This is a long-term commitment. Humane societies and shelters are filled with homeless animals—homeless through no fault of their own— victims of impulse decisions that were made and later regretted.

WHERE TO FIND THE BASSET OF YOUR DREAMS

When choosing your new dog, remember rule Number One: All Bassets are cute and lovable, but all those lovable dogs won't fit into that initial picture you drew in your mind. Only one will. And you'll know him when he comes along.

The second rule? Be patient! Explore all the possibilities and don't let your heart make a decision your mind knows is wrong. And the most important rule to remember? It's that choosing a good source for a puppy is as important as choosing the right puppy. You could find your beloved pet in many places—breeders, rescues, pet stores, and sometimes even shelters. It's important to do your homework and understand the pros and cons of each of these sources.

Breeders

Newspapers are filled with advertisements for "Basset Hound puppies. Champion Bloodlines." Screen these breeders carefully. Anyone who has to habitually advertise in newspapers to sell puppies is possibly just raising dogs for profit. Or, perhaps they wanted to have a litter of puppies for the kids to see firsthand the "miracle of birth." In either situation, the resulting puppies will be more likely to have genetic health problems than puppies bred by a professional breeder who has more than a basic understanding of genetics and is aware of the genetic problems that may lurk in her dog's bloodlines. A casual breeder (sometimes called a

Genetic Testing for Basset Hounds

Although Basset Hounds are generally healthy dogs in comparison to other breeds, several genetic health problems are possible in the breed. The more common genetic disorders reported in Basset Hounds include glaucoma, thrombopathy (blood platelet disorder), von Willebrand's disease (blood protein disorder), hypothyroidism, patellar luxation (slipped stifles), hip dysplasia, and elbow dysplasia. The BHCA encourages responsible breeding through the screening of breeding stock for genetic or inheritable health problems. No matter where you purchase your Basset, the evidence of these screenings should be available for both the parents of any puppy or adult you consider purchasing. Some of the testing suggested by the BHCA includes (but is not limited to):

- Gonioscopy. This is an eye examination checking specifically for signs of glaucoma, performed by a veterinary ophthalmologist. Results are registered with the Canine Eye Registration Foundation (CERF).

- Thrombopathia platelet aggregation studies. Currently, the availability of this test is very limited.

- Von Willebrand's factor antigen testing.

- Thyroid testing.

- Radiographs (x-rays) of hips and elbows with evaluation by a recognized registry (e.g., Orthopedic Foundation for Animals [OFA], PennHip, Institute for Genetic Disease Control in Animals [GDC], Ontario Veterinary College [OVC].)

- Temperament evaluation, as evidenced by Puppy Aptitude Testing or American Temperament Test Society, Inc. [ATTS] certification.

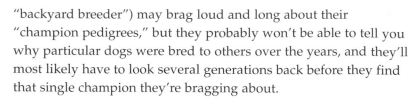

"backyard breeder") may brag loud and long about their "champion pedigrees," but they probably won't be able to tell you why particular dogs were bred to others over the years, and they'll most likely have to look several generations back before they find that single champion they're bragging about.

Finding a Responsible Breeder

Responsible, dedicated, and reputable breeders usually can be found through the local kennel club, from area veterinarians, or simply through word-of-mouth from friends. Go to a dog show or obedience trial and, if you see a Basset you like, ask the owner if they might have puppies or an older dog available. You may have to wait several months, or be put on a waiting list for those puppies, since responsible breeders don't overbreed their dogs. You won't get instant gratification, but you will more than likely end up with a healthy pet. You also can search the Internet for breeders from every corner of the world, although on the Internet, as well as in real life, breeders with bad or misguided intent must be weeded out from the truly dedicated professionals.

You'll know instantly when you come across a dedicated breeder. She'll have just as many questions for you as you have for her. These questions will likely include:

- Have you owned a dog in the past?
- Have you owned a Basset before?
- Why did you choose a Basset now?
- Do you know this breed's faults, as well as their good points?
- Do you have a fenced yard?
- Can you provide references from your veterinarian?
- Will you be willing to spay or neuter your pet?

Don't think you can get around these questions with half-truths or false statements. The dog world is a tightly knit network filled with breeders from around the country, and now—with the Internet providing a way to keep in touch at the touch of a button—around the world. And these breeders stay in close contact with each other. If you tell a breeder that you have a fenced yard, you'd better have one! Even if you live across the country from this breeder, her friend who breeds Boxers or Collies or Dachshunds may live just across town from you, and she may be more than willing to drive by to check out your place.

A reputable, conscientious breeder will not sell a puppy under 7

Good Temperament

The Basset Hound Club of America believes that good temperament is important in any Basset and "poor temperament is as debilitating as any serious genetic disorder."

(and some say up to 12) weeks of age, because early separation
from the dam and litter mates can be permanently detrimental both
psychologically and physically to a puppy. In fact, many states
have laws in place that make it illegal to sell a puppy any earlier
than at 8 weeks of age.

One advantage to purchasing your Basset from a good breeder
is that you can meet the mother (dam) and sometimes the father
(sire) or the litter. This is one of the best ways to check for
temperament. You should be able to pet the parent(s) and the
puppy, scratch their ears, and pick up their feet without any fear of
being nipped. If any of them should snap at you, quickly thank the
breeder for their time and don't let the door hit you on the way
out! There is no excuse for offering for sale any dog or puppy with
an unstable temperament. This is also the time to check over the
pups to make sure they look healthy—coughing, runny eyes, or an
overly rounded belly could spell trouble.

The responsible breeder won't actively try to sell you a dog or

Rescuing an older Basset can be extremely rewarding.

puppy. They'll try very hard to match you with the right puppy, and they won't be afraid to send you elsewhere if they don't think they have what you're looking for. They won't try to talk you into something you're not sure you want. They'll be able to offer pictures of several generations of their (mostly champion) dogs, and they'll show you a pedigree that they can explain in full, possibly even pulling out photo albums filled with photos of those ancestors that they've bred and shown and loved through the years.

Questions to Ask the Breeder

You should ask certain questions of any breeder from whom you're considering purchasing a dog. Any reputable breeder should not only be happy to answer your questions in full, but should be impressed that you cared enough to ask. These questions may include:

Make sure you have all of your puppy's supplies purchased before you bring him home.

- What types of problems might Bassets have, including genetic health problems? (A good breeder will have done all necessary genetic testing on her breeding stock and will be willing to share the results with you.)

- Has the litter been temperament tested? (This is the best way for a breeder to be able to place each puppy in a home where he will be most appreciated and valued.)
- What if I decide I can't keep my Basset? (Most breeders are willing to take the puppy or dog back if he does not work out in your home—most will even insist that this be part of the contract).
- What is the difference between your "show quality," "obedience prospect," or "pet" puppies?
- What kind of paperwork comes with my Basset? (There should be a contract stating what both parties can expect from the transaction. Your breeder also will give you not only the registration application for the puppy [or registration certificate for an older dog], but also will include a three- or four-generation pedigree and concise written instructions on how to take care of your new pet.)
- Are the puppy's vaccinations and health checks up to date?
- Do you belong to the national Basset breed club?
- Are you active in area dog clubs and events?
- May I call you with any questions after I've brought my Basset home? (A good breeder should become your mentor into the wonderful world of Bassets.)

Be wary of any breeder (or other person trying to sell you a dog) who doesn't add up!

Rescue Me!

Almost all purebred dog breeds have national, regional, and local rescue organizations that foster animals that have fallen upon hard times and are in need of help in finding a new home. You can check with a group like the Basset Hound Club of America who will be happy to help you find a rescue group in your area, as well as give you further information about this breed that you've chosen.

Don't think you're taking second choice by adopting an older or rescue dog or puppy. Dogs of all ages become available for adoption for dozens of reasons. They range from the sad (death of their owner), to the uneducated ("he sheds," "he needs too much attention," "he is too expensive"), to the ridiculous ("he no longer matches our home décor," "he isn't cute and cuddly any more, we want a new puppy.") We live in a disposable society where everything from diapers to razor blades are made for a one-time use. Sadly, this thinking goes beyond the department store and into the mind of many uneducated or irresponsible prospective pet owners.

Because puppies are cute, people easily forget what they're going to have when that sweet little cuddly ball of fur becomes an adult. When little Fluffy becomes too big, too active, or too dominant or hyperactive because of a lack of training, or simply when the novelty of owning a pet wears off, these owners often take the easy way out and dump him at the local shelter (or even worse, in the countryside), and drive away believing that their castoff will find a new home. Sadly, that is rarely the case, and very few abandoned pets actually do find good responsible homes. You'll find it more rewarding than you could ever imagine giving one of these abandoned pets a new chance at life.

Obviously, an older dog may come to you with problems that caused him to end up looking for a new home in the first place. Find out as much about the prospective adoptee as possible. Make sure he's healthy, or has health problems that are easily treatable. Also be certain that you have the time and patience to work through any training or temperament problems that may arise. Be sure that you are getting this dog through a reputable source that will be honest with you about his problems.

Some problems should not be acceptable. A dog who habitually bites humans should not be brought into a home with small children, and he should be evaluated carefully by a professional to see if he is adoptable into any home situation. A dog who barks obsessively should not be adopted by someone who is not home for long periods of time throughout the day. The very busy, hyperactive dog should be avoided if you live alone in an apartment; he needs a home with a large fenced yard and a large family to keep him entertained.

BRINGING HOME YOUR BASSET

It's time! Your Basset is old enough to come home and become a member of the family. Suddenly, the panic sets in. Much in the way that a first-time parent suddenly realizes the enormity of their

To make sure you're ready for your Basset, you must completely puppy-proof your home.

situation as they enter the delivery room in the obstetrics ward at the hospital, the first-time puppy owner is now faced with the realization that they are about to take on a long-term, full-time commitment.

If you're getting your puppy from a breeder, a week or so before your puppy arrives, it's a great idea to have each member of the family wear an old T-shirt for a day and then use these articles of clothing to stuff a small pillowcase. Send the breeder this pillow (securely zipped into a plastic bag to keep the scents intact) for the puppy to sleep with for a few days before your impending visit. Hopefully, by the time you arrive, the puppy will already recognize you and your family by your scent and feel comfortable with your taking him away from his home. Putting this pillow in the crate with him at his new home will help to make him feel comfortable and safe.

Puppy Proofing

To make sure you're ready for the new arrival, you must completely puppy-proof your home. You'll be amazed at how very much your puppy's actions will resemble those of a rambunctious human toddler, so if your house is already toddler-proof, you're a step ahead of the game. If it's not toddler proof, get to work!

Try to see your house from your puppy's perspective. Get down on all fours (or lower) and look around the room. Suddenly, all sorts of menacing objects come to view, especially electric and phone cords that can cause a nasty shock or even death if chewed. Cigarette and cigar butts in an ashtray look pretty innocuous, but can quickly create nicotine poisoning in a small animal. The chocolate candy that rolled under the couch at your last party could mean a stomach upset or worse, if found by a snooping puppy.

Obviously, any small knick-knacks that could be swallowed and prove a choking hazard should be moved to a higher shelf, and anything that won't be improved with puppy tooth-marks should be either removed or moved to a higher location. Once the puppy arrives, you'll quickly learn not to leave clothing, shoes, socks, belts, and other assorted pieces of clothing lying about, because

Purchase chew toys appropriate to your Basset's size.

Toy Don'ts

Your Basset's toy chest should not contain any of the following items:

- Items with hard, sharp points or attachments that can break off and be dangerous if swallowed.

- Shoes or other personal clothing. Offering these items to your puppy will confuse him, by teaching him that it's okay sometimes to chew your shoes and rip holes in your shirts.

- Balls of string, small balls, cellophane, small plastic bags, and other small items that could get lodged in your puppy's throat and cause him to choke or suffocate.

- Children's toys made of soft rubber, fur, wool, sponge, or plastic that could be chewed into small pieces.

your puppy will be especially attracted to them because they smell like his beloved family. As a canine humorist once wrote "the first thing [our puppy] did on arriving at our house was to eat a broom which upset his stomach, and then began devouring my best belt, which upset me!"

It's a good idea to not allow your puppy the full run of your home until he is trained. Baby gates and other barriers are worth their weight in gold to the puppy owner, because they effectively keep the puppy out of unpuppy-proofed areas. It's also wise to contain the puppy in a room with linoleum, vinyl, or other easy-to-clean floor covering. Many a carpet has not only been irreparably stained during potty training, but also shredded beyond repair by an unruly canine youngster with time on his paws.

Not only must your house be puppy-proofed but your yard as well. If your dog will have access near your driveway, be sure you check your cars for radiator leaks. Antifreeze is deadly to animals in even minute doses, and the sweet smell is very attractive to dogs.

If you have a nut tree in your yard, make sure all the nuts have been picked up, because they can be a choking hazard. Bottles and bags of yard and garden fertilizers and insecticides and other poisons should be kept out of the puppy's reach, and he shouldn't be allowed into any area that has been recently treated with any of these products. Many flower bulbs and common landscaping plants are poisonous to animals if ingested. Check your fence for cracks or holes, and be sure that the fencing material not only meets the ground, but also preferably goes beneath the soil level.

Avoid Chocolate

Chocolate is poisonous to dogs, and even small amounts can cause severe health problems, even death.

Supplies

Once you think your home and property is safe (and trust me, you only think it's safe; it's amazing what a baby puppy can find in a supposedly safe environment) it's time for the fun part—shopping for goodies for your new family member-to-be! Your puppy will possibly come to you with a packet of information as well as toys, food, and other items, so it's always a good idea to check with the puppy's current owner first to see what things you'll need to purchase.

Crate

The most important thing on the checklist is a crate or kennel. Although many people believe that using a crate for a dog is cruel, nothing could be further from the truth—if it's used responsibly. Because dogs in the wild are pack animals that live in a den, your Basset's kennel or crate quickly becomes his den—a safe place where he knows he won't be disturbed while he's eating or sleeping. You should reinforce this fact to your children so that they learn to respect the dog's private time-outs.

Many varieties of crates are on the market, including those constructed of hard molded plastic, wire, metal, and wood. Your choice should depend on your lifestyle and what would be more comfortable for your dog. Wire crates have good visibility, ventilation, and are easy to clean. Plastic dog crates are more lightweight, offer greater safety from the elements, and many are airline approved, making them popular with people who travel with their dogs. Folding crates such as those made by Nylabone have the added value and convenience of being easy to store away when not in use. Metal and wood crates usually are not cost effective for the pet owner.

The puppy should not be confined continuously (except at night) and will soon learn to quietly tolerate short bouts of confinement. Besides the obvious benefits of using a crate at home, having a pet that is unafraid of being crated or caged will make trips to the vet and groomer much less traumatic for everyone concerned. When you travel, it will make you much more welcome at hotels and motels if the manager can be assured that your pet will be crated when unsupervised.

Collar and Leash

You'll also need a collar and leash for your puppy. A flat or rolled buckle collar (not a slip or choke) collar is best. Collars come in myriad colors and materials, including leather, nylon, and cotton. Choosing the right one is not only a matter of personal preference, but must also take into consideration what will work best with your dog's lifestyle. Nylon is durable and good for active dogs. Leather collars are also sturdy and attractive, but cost more than nylon. Cotton is lightweight and comfortable, but not as sturdy as nylon or leather. You'll want to make sure ID tags are attached to the collar to help identify your puppy in case he is ever lost. We'll talk more about choosing the right collar for your Basset in Chapter 6. Because Bassets are prone to neck and back injury, a harness may be a good idea instead of a collar when you go for walks, especially if your Basset hasn't been trained to not pull against the leash.

A lightweight or retractable leash is necessary for keeping your Basset attached to you. Some retractable leashes come with a flashlight on the handle, which makes nighttime walks safer and more pleasant.

Food

You'll have to purchase puppy food for your new addition. Remember to purchase the brand your puppy has been fed up to this point. You'll also want to stock up on some treats for early training incentive.

You'll also need something to store your Basset's food in. Although dry kibble usually has a shelf life of up to one year after it is manufactured, that doesn't mean it will maintain its quality once the bag has been opened. Oxygen entering a bag of food will immediately begin to destroy the quality, because air oxidizes the good fats and vitamins that your dog needs for continued good health. Moisture can immediately begin to grow mold, which can be invisible and tasteless to your dog, but can be deadly. Bugs, mice, and other pests will see an open bag of dog food as an invitation to party. How to avoid these problems? Buy a plastic container with a tight fitting lid and, as soon as you open the food, put it inside this container, bag and all. Contact with plastic containers can leach vitamin C from the food, and the plastic itself can leach into the food.

Holiday Tip

Major holidays may not be a good time to bring a new puppy or other pet into your home. The stress and trauma of a new home is hard enough on a puppy or dog without factoring in extra company, overly excited youngsters, and all the rest of the trimmings that come with Christmas, birthdays, Easter, and other holiday celebrations.

Food and Water Bowls

You'll need dishwasher-safe nonchewable bowls—one each for food and water. A vast selection of styles and colors are available. You should find bowls that will not tip and are easy to clean, since they need to be washed daily. Most Basset owners find stainless steel works best.

Grooming Supplies

You'll need a guillotine-type nail trimmer, a firm bristle or rubber brush, a hound glove, and good quality pet shampoo and conditioner.

ID Tags and Microchipping

Because you love your pet, you'll want to do everything you can to keep him safe. He will have city tags if he lives in town, rabies vaccination tags no matter where he lives, and possibly even a tag with his name and phone number on it. Even with these precautions, you have no guarantee that he won't end up lost. Collars are easily lost or removed, and then your pet is unrecognizable from any other Basset Hound—unless your pet is microchipped!

Although it sounds like something from a sci-fi movie, microchipping is definitely the wave of the present in tracking down lost pets. No more painful than a vaccination, a tiny capsule about the size of a grain of rice is injected under the flap of skin on the back of the dog's neck. Veterinarians and shelters are provided with scanners that read the digital number on the chip inside the capsule. This number can then be cross-referenced with your name and address. A microchip is permanent (although sometimes they can "travel" beneath the skin and be difficult to locate), and it cannot be removed or altered.

A flat buckle collar will work well for your Basset.

Toys

Of course, you mustn't forget the fun stuff either. Your new puppy will need chew toys to take his mind off all the things you won't want him to chew. Make sure you get toys appropriate to his size. Nylabone makes toys that are suitable for a Basset's size and chewing power.

Other Items

During the housetraining stage, puppy piddle sheets are helpful if you decide to paper train before teaching him to go outside. A poop-scooper will come in handy on your walks. Also, while you're at the pet store, maybe you'll find yourself a cute T-shirt that proclaims "I Love My Basset Hound" or perhaps a coffee mug or mouse-pad for your desk with a similar sentiment.

The First Day

You should plan the trip to pick up your new puppy early in the day, so that he will have time to get acquainted with his new family well before bedtime. The first night in new surroundings is the hardest, and it will be easier on him if he already feels comfortable in this new situation.

If most of the family is gone during weekdays, plan on bringing the puppy home early on Saturday morning, so that you have all weekend to get to know each other before he has to be left alone on Monday morning. Ideally, choose a minor holiday weekend so that you can have an extra day to spend together.

When you go to pick up your puppy, you should pack a tote bag with items guaranteed to make the transition to a new home easier on the puppy. You'll need to pack towels (both cloth and paper), since the puppy is likely to get carsick or have an accident during the ride; treats; a chew toy; a squeaky toy; and maybe a large stuffed animal to remind him of his mom and litter mates. It's a good idea to not go alone on this monumental event. Someone will need to either hold or keep an eye on your little bundle of joy during the ride in case he gets sick or starts getting overly nervous. Try to keep the ride as calm as possible. Whether he rides in a crate or on the lap of someone in the back seat (riding in the front seat is never a good idea for dogs, unless no air bag is present on the passenger side) is a matter of personal preference. Certainly, the ride home can be a bonding time, but a dog is always safer when in his crate. Of course, if he won't lie quietly on someone's lap, he should immediately go into his crate.

Toy Tips

Keep an eye on your Basset's toys as he chews them. If a plush squeaky toy is ripped open by an exuberant chewer, the squeaker could pose a choking hazard. Also, be wary of any toys that can break or splinter.

Introduction Time

Remember, when you bring your new dog home for the first time, he is going to feel very bewildered and stressed by all the changes going on in his life. Be very careful not to surround him with too many people or overwhelm him with attention. Let him wander through your home uninterrupted, getting used to all the sights, smells, and sounds of his new surroundings. You should delay any introductions to anyone who doesn't actually live in the house with you until your Basset has had a chance to acclimate himself and consider his new surroundings "home."

To Other Pets

If you already have animals that live with you, introducing the newcomer will take a little bit of public relations work on your part to make sure that all goes smoothly and they become the best of friends.

If you're introducing a new puppy to an older pet, you must

Don't overwhelm your puppy on his first day home.

take great pains that the puppy doesn't get scared or hurt during the introduction. Be sure your original pet knows that he isn't being replaced, and give him lots of extra attention and treats.

If you're introducing a new older pet, you can expect some grumblings and protestations, but allow the animals to work things out on their own. Only interfere if it appears that there might be actual bloodshed. Keep treats handy for both, so that they see the introduction of the other as a positive experience, but don't allow the treats to become an issue that might prompt a fight. Be certain that you stay relaxed and happy. Your original pet will be carefully reading your demeanor, so if you appear apprehensive and worried, he will likely think it is a feeling caused by the "interloper," and he may try to "protect" you.

Riding in a Pickup Truck

If you are traveling in a pickup truck, your dog always should ride up front with you. On rare occasions when this may not be possible (and I can't think of any good reason why he wouldn't be welcome in the cab, unless he got too up close and personal with a skunk or a dead fish on one of your excursions), he should either be confined in a well-secured crate or tethered in the center of the vehicle. You should be aware that, in many states, it is illegal for a dog to ride loose in the back of a vehicle, both for his own safety's sake as well as that of those with whom you share the road.

To Children

If you have children, make sure they don't fight over whose time it is to hold the puppy. He's not a stuffed toy that they can play tug-of-war with. Remember that even small children appear large and frightening to a baby puppy (or an older dog who has been exposed to the seamier side of life), especially since children are more prone to making loud noises and sudden movements than are most adults.

Never leave your children alone with a new dog, especially a young puppy or a rescue dog who may have issues of which you're unaware. Even older children and those well trained on how to behave around dogs shouldn't be left alone with your pets. Remember, dogs are not babysitters, and kids don't always use good judgment when dealing with animals. Be aware, and always supervise.

HOW TO TRAVEL WITH YOUR BASSET

More and more dog owners are traveling with their dogs. Whether you've decided to take your Basset with you on the family trip to the Grand Canyon, or are just transporting him to the vet for his yearly checkup, here are some tips that can make traveling with your pooch safe and fun.

In the Car

Letting your dog run loose in the car isn't a good idea. Dogs can easily escape when a door opens and they see something or someone that they want to greet outside. Also, in the case of an accident (which an unruly dog riding loose in a car can easily cause), he will be much more likely to suffer serious injuries than if he was restrained. The safest place for your dog during car travel is either in a carrier or a restraining harness that works with the car's seat belt to keep him securely in his place. Remember that the passenger seat is not a good place for your dog to ride, because he could easily be killed by the air bag deploying in case of an accident. Air bags were designed for the average-sized adult, sitting 20 inches (50.8 cm) or more from the dashboard. A dog's head is much lower than a human's and may be much closer to the dash. Since an air bag deploys at 200 mph (32km/hr), you can imagine how much damage it can do to a dog.

Never leave your dog unattended in the car, even in cool weather. Even the winter sun can warm up a car's interior to uncomfortable levels in a surprisingly short time. And the summer sun can raise the heat to lethal levels.

Make sure you supervise your children with the new dog.

If your road trip is a long one, remember to bring his food and water from home. You should plan to stop often to let him stretch his legs and go potty. Don't forget to bring either a poop scooper or plastic bags to clean up after him.

By Air

Most airlines will accept dogs on their flights, although few will allow them to ride with passengers (except puppies and small breeds that can fit in a small crate beneath the seat). Since your Basset is a large breed, he'll have to ride as cargo. Here are some tips for traveling by air with your Basset:

Pet Politics

When introducing yuor new pet to an older one, you may want to have them meet for the first time outside your home in "nuetral" territory your old pet won't see as his own.

- Be sure you call ahead to check your specific airline's specifications for shipping a Basset, and be certain you show up with the correctly sized crate.
- Let the airline know well ahead of time that you will be bringing a dog, as some airlines only allow a certain number of animals per flight.
- You will need to check in earlier than usual, to allow for the extra time required to get your pet checked in.
- The baggage area can be a noisy, scary place, so it's a good idea to place cotton balls in your Basset's ears to make things a little quieter for him.
- You can discuss with your vet the advisability of using a mild sedative, but this may not be a wise choice unless you are certain how it will affect your dog. Remember, no one will be watching him for several hours.
- Give him a favorite toy, a soft blanket, and something to chew on during his flight.
- Your veterinarian must check out your pet within a week of your trip and will give you a certificate that is necessary before your dog will be accepted on any airline.

Hotel or Motel

If you plan to stay overnight in a hotel, be sure you advise them ahead of time that you will be bringing a dog with you. You can check websites like www.dogfriendly.com or www.petswelcome.com to find a hotel along your route that is dog-friendly. Remember that you and your dog are ambassadors for all people who travel with their pets. Make sure that when you leave, you leave everything as you find it. Bring a sheet or blanket from home to cover the bedspread if your dog sleeps with you. Clean up after your pet when he goes to the bathroom (indoor accidents as well as outside). If any damage is done while you're there, own up to it and make restitution.

If your Basset will be left alone in the room, put him in his crate, put a "Do Not Disturb" sign on the door, and leave the TV or radio turned on—not only as company for him, but to mask any noise he might make that would irritate neighbors. Always advise the maids that a crated dog is in the room if you will be gone during a time when the room might be cleaned.

WHEN YOU CAN'T TAKE YOUR BASSET WITH YOU

Although you'll always want your Basset beside you, there may be times when he will not be allowed to travel with you. In those cases, it's imperative that you find a good pet sitter or a boarding kennel that you can trust.

Boarding Kennel

Ask friends or your veterinarian for kennel recommendations. Before boarding your Basset, visit the kennel. It should be clean, filled with friendly staff and happy dogs. Make sure that you do a thorough check of every aspect of your dog's daily care before you leave your Basset in their hands. Some boarding kennels offer doggie day care, where you can drop off your Basset for a set amount of hours during the day. Doggie day care can be a great option for people who work long hours—their Basset will be fed and exercised appropriately, and more importantly, he won't be lonely. Doggie daycare is also a great way to get

Kennel Tip

Before you leave your Basset Hound with a boarding kennel, check them out with the American Boarding Kennel Association (www.abka.com) to see if they are approved.

your dog acclimated to the kennel before you must leave him there while you're away.

Make sure to leave your Basset with someone you trust when you can't take him with you.

Pet Sitters

If you can't take your Basset with you and opt against the kennel option, you can always ask a family member or friend to Basset-sit for you. Or, you can hire a professional pet sitter who will very ably take care of things while you're gone.

Always check the references of anyone you will be trusting your Basset (and your home) with. It might be a good idea to also do a criminal record check (available for a nominal fee online). If you have problems finding a local sitter, you can call the National Association of Professional Pet Sitters at 1-800-296-PETS. Be sure to leave contact numbers while you're gone, including numbers where you can be reached and contact numbers for emergency situations. Create a detailed care sheet for every aspect of your Basset's care well ahead of time, so that you can be sure he'll be well taken care of while you are away.

FEEDING
Your Basset Hound

hen you ask the question, "What should I feed my Basset?" be prepared for many different replies, depending upon who you ask. While one person may swear by the Bones and Raw Food diet (affectionately, if not appetizingly referred to as BARF), another by home-cooked preparations, and still another by feeding the highest quality of prepackaged dog kibble, they will all agree that no matter what you feed your Basset, don't overdo it.

Obesity is a common complaint within the Basset world, because this breed is extremely food oriented. One breeder says she swears she could teach her Basset to walk on water if she used enough liver bits. While this works to your benefit during training time, it makes it hard to make sure that your Basset keeps to his diet. Bassets are consummate "counter surfers," and they almost seem to be able to levitate to reach foodstuffs that you were certain you had shoved far enough back on the countertop to be out of reach.

Let's take a look at all the food options available to you to keep your Basset healthy and at his ideal weight.

COMMERCIAL FOOD

Walk into any pet store and you'll be astounded by the array of choices for prepackaged foods. You have your choice of dry food (also called kibble), canned food, and semi-moist food. The quality of commercial food can vary greatly, so it's very important to read the label to make sure you are feeding your Basset a high-quality diet. Despite the bad rap some prepackaged food gets from holistic and homeopathic pet owners, you can't argue with its convenience and availability. Just remember that dogs must have the right balance of nutrients, (i.e., proteins, fats, carbohydrates, vitamins, and minerals), and they must be in a form that is digestible by the dog.

Reading the Label

Pet food labels are regulated by rules different from those for foods for human consumption, but reading and understanding a pet food label can help you make informed food choices for your pets.

The product name is the first part of the label that any consumer notices, and the name can be a key factor in the decision to buy a product, especially if you aren't educated in reading and understanding the actual ingredients. Be a savvy shopper and pet owner, learn what marketing ploys are used to sell dog food, and don't fall for gimmicky names and advertisements. Choose the highest quality dog food you can afford, and feed it at a proper ratio for your dog as recommended by your vet, not what the bag of food suggests. Every animal has a different level of activity, metabolism, and ambient environmental temperature. In addition, breed, age, and other environmental stresses all impact daily requirements. Use the feeding guidelines on the bag of kibble as a rough starting point. If your animal becomes thin, feed him more often and/or in greater quantity. If your pet is obese, feed him less.

Watch the Treats

Help keep your Basset's weight in check. When feeding your dog, be sure to factor in the number of treats he is given during the day, as well as the food he's managed to steal that wasn't on his menu.

Ingredients to Look Out For

In addition to learning the percentage of fat and protein in a bag of kibble, a list of ingredients should be displayed on the label. The order of those ingredients is of vital importance to the consumer—and to your dog.

You want to see a specific type of protein with the word "meal" as the first ingredient. The type of meat should be spelled out—not a generic "meat meal," but chicken, lamb, pork, or beef meal. Be sure it says "meal" after the type of meat. Whole meat is mostly water, so if you don't get meat meal, your dog is being cheated. For what it's worth, when choosing your pet food, consider that most nutritionists prefer a chicken-based diet, because dogs tend to digest chicken better than lamb or beef.

Also look for the by-products on the label, which are usually heads, necks, stomach contents, organs, and other less desirable parts. Although these items sound disgusting to humans, in the wild, these are the first parts of a fresh kill that a dog will eat. It may sound distasteful to eat animal organs, but they are higher in natural vitamins and minerals than other parts of the carcass. Just make sure that the "by-product" is specific in its type and not listed as just "meat" or "poultry" by-product. You should know if it is chicken, lamb, beef, or some other meat source.

Because corn is usually one of the cheapest products to include in pet foods, you may see some type of corn product in the food. Some dogs can tolerate and process corn easily, others can't. If your dog starts itching, licking his feet, getting ear infections, or showing other types of allergic reactions, and the food you feed has corn in it, this may be a signal that your dog isn't tolerating the corn. Wheat also tends to be an allergen with many dogs, as does soy. Remember that, when reading labels, although a meat meal may be the first ingredient on the list (meaning it is the primary ingredient) the cereals and vegetables still could be added together and become the primary ingredient. You should be certain that the food you choose does not change its recipe according to which grains are cheaper during particular times of the year.

You also should look for a food that has no chemical preservatives (ethoxyquin, BHA, BHT, or propyl gallate) listed on the label. Instead, look for food that is preserved with mixed tocopherols (vitamin E). You should be aware that a dog food company does not have to list any preservative that the company

It's very important to make sure you are feeding your Basset a high-quality diet.

itself did not add: The ingredients used in preparing the kibble may have been treated with chemical preservatives at another company before going into that particular food.

You should never choose a dog food that is unnaturally colored to make it more palatable to the human who is serving it. Dogs don't care what color their food is—they just care about the taste, smell, and texture. Some colorings can not only be harmful to dogs, but can cause discoloration of hair.

What Type of Commercial Food Is Best for My Basset?

If you decide on commercial food, most Basset owners feed their dogs kibble. A diet that consists mainly of canned food isn't recommended, since canned food tends to include extra sugars to make it more palatable. Also, eating dry kibble can help keep a dog's teeth strong and healthy.

What type of commercial food is best? It depends on his age, size, and if he has any special needs. Puppy food is richer in protein, fat, vitamins, and minerals (especially calcium and phosphorous) than adult food. It is calculated to meet the rapid growth and metabolic rate of an active, maturing puppy. (Puppy food also is suggested for pregnant or lactating females.) Although most puppy food manufacturers and many breeders and veterinarians recommend keeping a young dog on puppy food for 12 to 18 months, a large contingent of veterinary researchers now recommend progressing to adult food as early as 4 to 6 months of age. These researchers believe that most prepackaged puppy food often is too nutrient dense and rich for dogs as they age, and it's been suggested that it may actually contribute to orthopedic problems (such as hip dysplasia, osteochondritis desiccans, and panosteitis), as well as obesity if continued for too long a time.

A popular consensus says that adult/maintenance diets are desirable for most dogs from the ages of 6 months to 6 to 8 years. After your Basset reaches the age of 8, a senior diet is suggested. Senior diets possess fewer calories, more fiber, and an electrolyte and nutritional balance more suitable for older dogs. You should consider switching to a food formulated for seniors when your dog reaches the age of 6 to 8 years, especially if he is less active or overweight.

If your dog is overweight or obese, lite diets contain fewer

Ethoquin Controversy

The jury is still out on how damaging the preservative ethoxyquin really is for your dog, but a lot of very well-researched literature is available on the subject. Do your homework, so that you can make your own educated and informed decision.

What AAFCO Statements on the Label Mean

When reading your dog food labels, look for a statement that "AAFCO (The Association of American Feed Control Officials) feeding trials confirm that [Name of Dog Food] is complete and balanced for adult dogs or all life stages." This means the food was actually fed to real dogs to determine that it meets the nutritional needs for your dog. Some food companies merely determine the nutritional values in their lab, without ever feeding it to actual dogs. Their label reads more like this: "[Name of Dog Food] has been shown to be complete and balanced using testing procedures as outlined by AAFCO."

If neither statement shows up on your bag of kibble, call the company and ask them whether their food was actually fed to dogs during an AAFCO-approved feeding trial, or whether the numbers simply added up correctly in their laboratory.

calories, less fat, and more fiber, and they also may contain fat absorbers or metabolic accelerators. Performance foods, the other end of the spectrum from lites, are very high in protein and fat and are only appropriate for dogs on a rigorous, regular training schedule that depletes the system faster than most regular foods can replenish it. This might apply to Bassets who participate in tracking, obedience, search and rescue, or field work. Make sure you ask your vet before switching your Basset to any of these special types of commercial food.

Make sure you supply your Basset with plenty of fresh water to drink.

Prepackaged foods also are available with formulas designated for large-breed dogs that typically contain higher levels of glucosamine and chondroitin to reduce the likelihood of joint maladies. Prescription diet foods also are available from veterinarians for dogs with various medical disorders, including endocrine, gastrointestinal, urinary, and cardiac conditions. A diet of regular prepackaged foods may aggravate these types of conditions.

Pros and Cons of the Commercial Diet

Pros:

- *Convenience.* No preparation is necessary with this diet. Just open the package and pour it into a bowl.
- *Availability.* An endless variety is available in pet stores, and almost every supermarket now carries even premium brand dog foods. You can pick up the dog's food when you're picking up yours.
- *Cost.* Although premium brand foods are more costly than nonpremium, they are still cheaper than purchasing foods to cook or serve raw.

Cons:

- *Health issues.* Additives, preservatives, and colors can create allergic reactions and skin irritations in some dogs. Cheaper brands may not have the proper balance of dietary needs for your Basset.
- *Cosmetics.* The coloring in some foods can put a stubborn stain on your dog's mouth and face hair.

BONES AND RAW FOODS (BARF) DIET

This diet (also known as Biologically Appropriate Raw Food) is based on feeding your dog whole, raw, natural foods, including whole raw bones. Proponents of the BARF diet claim that this diet produces much healthier dogs than those fed commercial diets. The basis behind this diet comes from the idea that dogs descended from wild pack animals who hunted for their food. Those dogs ate only the game they could catch and vegetable matter they found palatable. Dr. Ian Billinghurst, a world-renowned veterinary surgeon and one of the greatest proponents of the raw foods diet, states firmly that "Sixty to eighty percent of a dog's diet should be

Raw Bones are Best

Always use raw bones, never cooked. A raw bone is not likely to splinter, whereas a cooked bone almost certainly will splinter — thus necessitating an emergency trip to the vet for costly, life-threatening abdominal surgery.

raw meaty bones."

If you decide to feed your dog the BARF diet, those who swear by it promise that you'll be amazed at how simple it is. Start with basics—a range of raw meaty bones, fish, eggs, and fresh fruits and vegetables. For the majority of raw feeders, chicken is the basis of the majority of their dog's meals. It's easy to come by, it's cheap, and it's good for the dog. If chicken isn't readily available to you, use what you can get locally—lamb, beef, venison, duck, rabbit, pig, or raw whole fish. As long as it is raw and meaty and came from a good processing source, it will be good for your dog.

Remember that your dog does not have the right digestive system to cope with a lot of grains, so don't include them in your raw diet. In addition to not digesting them well, grains are the biggest source of allergies in dogs. Since grains make up the

You can find commercial foods made specifically for large-breed dogs.

majority of a lot of prepackaged dog foods, that's another reason to consider feeding an all-raw diet. You might also consider whether the beef you feed your dog was feedlot (grain) raised, or grass-fed. For both humans and animals, beef from a grass-fed cow provides a healthier meat. Most processors don't mark their beef as grain- or grass-fed, but some will be able to tell you if you ask them.

An added benefit to feeding the BARF diet is that your dog will require fewer trips to the dentist for teeth cleaning. Most dogs who need regular dental cleanings are fed soft moist dog food or dry kibble which, unlike feeding bones, doesn't clean off the plaque buildup on your dog's teeth.

Many people hesitate about feeding raw foods and eggs to their dogs, because they have heard warnings about bacterial contamination. Although those warnings are applicable to humans, they don't apply to dogs. A healthy dog's stomach acid is exceptionally strong (think about the kinds of things a wild dog eats) and is designed by nature to break down and destroy the bacteria that a human stomach could never tolerate. Also, the intestinal tract of the dog is short and designed to move food quickly and efficiently, giving it less time to cause problems.

Pros and Cons of the BARF Diet

Pros:

- *Health.* A natural raw diet has been proven in many cases to eliminate some dog food–related problems such as anal gland impaction, heavy plaque buildup on teeth, skin problems, allergic reactions, and weight problems. The overall condition of dogs usually improves; muscle mass, coat condition, and energy levels are usually much better when dogs are fed a proper BARF diet.
- *No additives.* You aren't feeding your dog the artificial preservatives and colors contained in many prepackaged dog foods. No rancid or questionable fats are included.
- *May reduce the chances of bloat.* The raw diet does not expand in the gut, which could possibly cause bloat, an extremely painful and potentially life-threatening problem to which some Bassets are prone.
- *Taste.* It is palatable to almost every dog.

Cons:

- *Switching.* If a dog has been raised on a kibble diet, the switch

must be done gradually to avoid problems with toxin release.

- *Less convenient.* Meat must be found, purchased, and stored properly. It must be thawed before feeding, which takes more forethought and time than opening a can or scooping food from a bag.
- *Cost.* The BARF diet is more expensive than a prepackaged commercial diet.
- *Traveling.* Traveling can be more difficult, since it is harder to carry or find a source for meats on the road.

You should ask your vet before you consider an all-raw diet for your dog. Also, go ahead and do your own research and ask questions of other vets, breeders, and owners.

HOMECOOKED DIET

In today's busy world, it's sometimes hard to find time to cook for the family, but a surprising number of people go a step further and cook for their dogs. By controlling their dogs' food, proponents of the homecooked diet believe that their dogs are healthier and that it is well worth the extra time and effort.

Certainly, more and more literature supports the fact that low-quality prepackaged foods can be harmful to our dogs for many reasons. By homecooking for your dog, you can avoid feeding too many grains and not enough meat products, and you can be sure no unwanted contents are included in the food, like harmful preservatives that may have a link to seizures as well as other health issues.

It's important to do your research and talk to your vet before embarking on a homecooked diet for your Basset.

It's important to do your research and talk to your vet before embarking on this type of diet for your dog. The proper balance of protein, vitamins, and minerals must be achieved to keep your Basset healthy.

What to Cook for Your Basset

The following recipe is suggested by a long-time dog owner who cooks 2 days a week for her dog, then freezes the food into daily serving amounts.

Doggy Stew

4 cups (1.8 kg) chicken, fish, or lean ground meat (about 2 pounds)

1 cup (.45 kg) zucchini or other fresh vegetable, finely chopped

1 cup (.45 kg) string beans, cut up

1/2 cup (.23 kg) white potato, cut up

1/2 cup (.23 kg) yam or sweet potato

4 cups (1.8 kg) water

Combine all ingredients in a slow cooker. Place on the lowest setting, and let it cook all day while you're at work or while you're sleeping. Place in the refrigerator to cool. Skim off any fat that accumulates on top. Mix together well and keep refrigerated or freeze in daily serving sizes.

You can mix and match the vegetables according to what's on sale at the grocery store or farmer's market, or what's available in your own garden. Dogs seem to especially love carrots, summer squash, green beans, and tomatoes.

Make sure you're feeding your puppy enough times during the day—feeding schedules for puppies are far different from those of an adult.

Tasty Homecooked Treats for Your Dog

Even if you decide that cooking for your dog's every meal is too much for your schedule, you can still incorporate some good home cooking into his diet with these tasty doggy treats. (Just be sure to label them "For the Dog"!)

Tasty Meatballs

You can double or triple (or quadruple, depending on your dog's appetite) this recipe and freeze any "leftovers" (if there are any).

1/2 pound (.23 kg) ground beef

1 carrot, finely grated

1/4 cup (.11 kg) of any other seasonal vegetable, grated

1 Tablespoon grated cheese (your dog's favorite flavor)

1/2 teaspoon garlic powder (powder, not salt!)

1/2 cup (.23 kg) whole wheat bread crumbs (make a piece of overdone toast and crumble it)

1 egg, beaten

1 tablespoon tomato paste

Combine all ingredients and mix well. Roll into small meatballs and place on a lightly greased cookie sheet. Bake in a preheated 350°F (177° C) oven until the meatballs are brown and firm (about 15 minutes). Cool completely, and store in an airtight container. Keep refrigerated.

Holy Mackerel Cakes

Not only is mackerel cheap, but it is a fabulous source of protein and calcium. The bones are left in the mackerel when it is canned, but they are very soft and chewy, and won't be a choking risk for your dog.

15 oz (.42 kg) can mackerel

1/2 cup (.45 kg) whole grain bread crumbs

1 teaspoon garlic powder (not garlic salt)

1 tablespoon minced green pepper

2 tablespoons vegetable or peanut oil

1 egg, beaten

Preheat the oven to 350°F (177° C). Using a fork, flake the mackerel and mash it thoroughly. Add the other ingredients and mix well. Shape into small balls and place on a greased cookie sheet. Using your fork, press each ball slightly to flatten it. Bake for about 20 minutes. Flip the cakes over and bake an additional five minutes to brown them on both sides and dry them out slightly. Cool completely and store in the refrigerator in an airtight container.

Sample Feeding Schedule

Puppies	Puppies	Adolescents	Adults
(6 to 12 weeks)	(12 weeks to 6 months)	(6 months to 1 year)	(1 year and up)
4 times a day	3 times a day	2 times a day	2 times a day

Pros and Cons of a Homecooked Diet

Pros:

- *Condition.* A dog's overall condition usually improves when fed a homecooked diet. In many cases, problems such as skin conditions, allergic reactions, and weight issues are eliminated when switched to a natural, homecooked diet.
- *Control.* You know you aren't feeding your Basset any artificial preservatives and colors with this diet.
- *Taste.* It is palatable to almost every Basset.

Cons:

- *Switching.* If your Basset has been on a prepackaged diet, the switch must be done gradually to avoid problems with toxin release.
- *Less convenient.* Foods must be purchased separately, then prepared and stored.
- *Time consuming.* Researching proper nutrition and cooking well-balanced meals for your Basset takes time.
- *Traveling may be difficult*, because it is harder to carry homecooked meals, or find a place on the road to cook them.

FEEDING SCHEDULES

As with so many other aspects of owning a dog, deciding on when to feed your Basset can bring up just as much debate as what to feed him. Ask your veterinarian and your breeder what dog food they suggest and what type of daily feeding schedule you should follow. Some might suggest free feeding, while others put their Bassets on a fixed feeding schedule. Free feeding means putting down a bowl of food and allowing your Basset to snack throughout the day. While this works for some dogs (usually in a single dog household), it isn't a good idea for a dog who bolts his food (eats it all at once very quickly), is a picky eater, or in a multiple dog household.

Most Basset owners find that feeding several meals a day on a fixed schedule works best. Some people feed their dogs only one meal a day, while some dogs are fed twice each day, in the morning and evening. Larger breeds such as the Basset benefit from smaller meals more often, to lessen the chances of bloat and to aid digestion.

Feeding schedules for puppies are far different from those of an adult. A 6- to 12-week-old puppy should be fed four times a day. (Your veterinarian can suggest any supplements he may need to get his body off to a good start.) At 12 weeks of age, you can begin feeding three meals a day, until he is 6 months old. From 6 months to a year, he should be fed twice a day. If the twice-a-day feeding works well with your schedule, and your dog is healthy, you might consider keeping up that schedule for life.

Varying the Schedule

Although it's a good idea to have some sort of schedule for feeding, be careful to vary the feeding times just a bit to avoid

As your Basset matures, make sure you are feeding him properly for his age and activity level.

creating too much of a creature of habit. Our dogs quickly adjust to a regular feeding schedule and specific food composition. This can create big trouble if you ever have to deviate from the schedule. If you feed your dog exactly the same food every day at 6 p.m., your dog's gastrointestinal system will soon program itself to start a digestion process at exactly that time. What does the dog's body do with all those excess digestive juices produced by the stomach at the programmed time? If you are even a few minutes late in getting your dog's food, he is likely to vomit those juices, which contain strong chemicals. Without any food to neutralize them, they can hurt the stomach. Not only is a change in schedule likely to adversely affect the dog on too strict a routine, but any minute change in food also can start gastrointestinal distress that can become very serious. Unfortunately, most inexperienced owners see this vomiting as further proof that their dog must adhere to his schedule even more strictly.

This doesn't mean you should feed at a different time of day each day, or feed your dog different foods every day. It just means that you should occasionally vary your feeding times and food, so that, in the case of an emergency when you can't feed exactly on time, or you run out of his regular kibble, or you don't have time to prepare homecooked or raw and you have to feed him prepackaged foods, you don't have a sick dog on your hands.

NUTRITION FOR THE SENIOR BASSET

The senior dog requires a special diet for maximum health and activity as their body undergoes changes related to aging. Because your Basset cannot easily digest fats during his senior years, great care must be taken to choose a diet that will contain the correct amount of calories to maintain his weight, without the addition of excess fats that can add to the problem of obesity. It's definitely worth the investment to purchase special dry foods formulated for the older pet. Small amounts of lean hamburger, cottage cheese, or yogurt are excellent additions to a senior pet's diet. Special foods may also need to be chosen to specifically treat diseases and ailments that affect many seniors, including heart and kidney failure. It's important that these foods only be given on the advice of a veterinarian, after a firm diagnosis has been made. Your vet also may suggest dietary supplements or vitamins

Feeding Tips for Your Basset

- Avoid feeding Basset Hounds fad diets.
- Pregnant females require more food and vitamins.
- Puppies should eat 3 to 4 meals a day in proportion to their size.
- It is better to feed an adult Basset Hound 2 to 3 meals a day rather than one large meal, because Bassets are prone to bloat.
- Bassets may get fat partly because their sad look tends to encourage their owners to give them more treats than they require.

to add years to your pet's life.

THE HEALTHY, WELL-FED BASSET

No matter which food you choose to feed to your Basset, you can tell whether your dog is getting the proper nutrition as long as you know what to look for. The way your Basset looks on the outside, plainly visible to the well-trained eye, mirrors the internal systems of your Basset. If you like what you see, you can be sure

Obesity can lead to many health problems, so keep an eye on your Basset's weight.

that your Basset is getting good nutrition, which is imperative for resisting infections and disease.

Check your Basset's eyes. If the membrane visible under the lower eyelid is light or white in color, it means he is not correctly assimilating nutrients or is receiving improper amounts of iron or other minerals in his diet. If the color is normal (pink to red), it means that he is receiving the correct balance and his body is using it properly.

Check your dog's gums and mouth tissue (both color and texture). If the gums are loose on the teeth, bleeding, light in color, or have white spots, it indicates that he is not receiving or assimilating proper amounts of vitamins, minerals, and amino acids. Normally, the gums are firm on the teeth, produce no bleeding when they're rubbed, and are a nice dark color. Vitamins and minerals also will affect your dog's energy and activity level, as well as muscle tone.

The skin is also a good indicator of nutritional balance. Improper balances of protein and fatty acids can make skin dry and flaky and can make the dog more prone to developing "hot spots." It also can make a Basset's coat dry, brittle, and dull in color. Good skin is soft, smooth, and pliable, with no signs of dandruff, flaking, or moist eczema. When checking the skin, you also should check for proper amounts of fluids. Without proper hydration, the skin hangs on the body, seems stiff, and when pulled away from the body, retains the shape without smoothing itself back down to the contours of the body.

THE OVERWEIGHT BASSET

Indiscriminate feeding habits play a large part in any dog's problem with weight. Feeding table scraps and low-quality food, providing constant access to food, and too many rich treats are significant contributing factors. Also, competitive eating in multiple dog households may be a factor not always apparent to the owner. Add in the fact that few dogs get the daily exercise they need, and it's no wonder that almost one-fourth of the dogs in the United States have problems with obesity.

Anatomy also influences weight gain in canines. Orthopedic conditions like hip dysplasia, osteoarthritis, cruciate ligament, and meniscal injury, which are acquired, developmental, or present at birth may reduce the ambulatory capacity of the animal and

The visible membrane under a healthy Basset's lower eyelid should be pink or red in color.

predispose him to pain, which keeps him from getting enough exercise to stay trim. Since some of these conditions actually can be caused by obesity, it is indeed a vicious circle.

Many canines gain weight from problems related to metabolism. Metabolic disorders including diabetes mellitus, hypothyroidism, hyperadrenocorticism (Cushing's disease), Addison's disease, and other endocrine abnormalities influence energy and metabolism. Animals suffering from one or more of these metabolic conditions often become overweight as a result of not having the energy to exercise and, even when they're forced to do so, not enough metabolic function to burn calories.

If your dog has a weight problem, your veterinarian may prescribe a high fiber/reduced calorie diet or advocate other

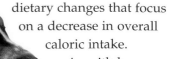

dietary changes that focus on a decrease in overall caloric intake.

As with humans, another method to manage weight is to increase exercise. If you feel your Basset is overweight, have him examined by a veterinarian and discuss the options available for safe and effective weight management. Untreated obesity can be a devastating condition for your pet; instituting a diet and exercise program may add quality (and years) to your Basset's life.

How Do I Know If My Basset Is Overweight?

Most owners find it hard to accurately judge if their dog has gained weight. Unlike humans, who have a love–hate affair with their bathroom scales, the only time a dog is weighed is when he visits the vet. If you have an otherwise healthy dog who only sees the veterinarian for annual or semi-annual vaccinations and checkups, he already may have developed a weight problem before you even realize it. Considering the health issues that go with obesity—whether as a cause or an effect—it's very important to keep a close eye on your dog's waistline.

Dogs Have Waists?

They should! Stand above your dog, look down, and check for his "waist." Bassets at the proper weight will have a visible indentation behind their ribs. Place both hands, palms down, lightly on your dog's ribs. You should be able to feel the ribs, but they should not be sticking out. If you cannot feel the ribs, chances are your dog is overweight. (If you can see the ribs, chances are your dog is underweight.) Overweight dogs also commonly have pouches of fat in the groin area between the hind legs.

What to Do if Your Dog Is Overweight

Obesity is probably the most common nutritional disease among adult dogs in Western countries. Few of us can afford a personal trainer to get our own waistlines back to normal, but your Basset should be able to count on you to get him back in shape.

- Cut out all treats and table snacks during the weight loss period (inappropriate or too many table scraps should always be a no-no, no matter whether your dog has a weight problem or not).
- Since the primary reason for obesity in dogs is overeating, divide his daily food allowance into two to four small meals a day. Never free-feed a dog who has a weight issue.
- Weigh your dog at the same time of day at least once a week, and keep a record of his weight. If you can pick up your Basset, simply step on the scales with him in your arms, note the weight, set him down, and weigh yourself alone—subtract the second number from the first, and you have your Basset's weight. If you can't pick up your dog, either call a strong friend to do it for you, or ask your vet or pet supermarket if you can borrow their scales for regular weigh-ins.
- If you have multiple dogs, feed them one at a time, in a crate,

Teach your dog to take treats gently from you.

or in separate rooms. A dieting dog will try to move to the bowl of his housemate to get more food.

• Feed your dog before you eat and keep him in another room during meals to discourage begging.

• Restrict your dog's unsupervised outdoor activity so that he may not scavenge for food when outside. Make sure that indoor and outdoor rubbish bins have secure covers, and that any food left for wild or outdoor animals is kept out of the reach of your Basset.

• Tell your neighbors and visiting friends about your dog's weight-loss program, so that they aren't tempted to feed him when he "complains" to them that he's starving.

• Always provide plenty of clean, fresh water.

• Exercise your dog on a regular basis. Start slowly, with short activity periods, and gradually increase the exercise time. Begin with walking and, when your pet shows signs of increased fitness, move to games that require running, such as fetch. You'll also find that the added exercise with your pet will help you maintain better health for yourself.

MIND YOUR MANNERS

Good table manners for your Basset doesn't just mean not letting him beg for food from your table, but also teaching him what is acceptable behavior whenever any food is involved. You should start teaching your puppy as early as possible to eat his food when it is put before him. The easy way to do this is to put the bowl in front of him, and keep it there as long as he is eating; when he walks away, pick it up and don't put it down again until his next mealtime. Soon, he will learn to eat when food is put before him. If he starts wolfing his food, put a large rock in the middle of his bowl, forcing him to eat around it, which should slow him down.

Teach your dog to take treats gently from you, and if he grabs at the treat, quickly take it away from him and try again later. Giving him a treat that you can hold tightly while he eats is a good way to teach him to take food gently. Don't turn it into a tug of war, but let him gently nibble off pieces.

Once he's learned the proper way to eat his own food, it's time to teach him the difference between your food and his. The easiest way to do this is to feed him in a different room than the one you eat in. Also, if you want to avoid begging, you shouldn't share your

human food with him. It doesn't take very much to teach your dog bad habits. Feeding him just once or twice from your table will teach him to expect it, and giving in to his pleading eyes and whimpers will reinforce the bad behavior. Even the unintentionally dropped food quickly scarfed up by an eager Basset can teach him to anticipate treats whenever his family is eating. Teach him early on that begging at the table will get him removed from the room or put outside.

Allowing your dog to beg at the table will make mealtimes with company especially uncomfortable for both you and your guests. You'll have to worry that they're feeding him inappropriate foods, and they'll likely worry that their clothes are going to be ruined by drool (Pavlov's dogs had nothing on a Basset eyeing his human's meals). Start young and be consistent with your training, and your dog should have excellent table manners and be welcomed into any situation.

An overweight dog should be supervised at all times while outside to prevent him from scavenging for food.

GROOMING

Your Basset Hound

hen someone mentions "grooming your dog," thoughts immediately flash to the spaniels, setters, poodles, terriers, and other breeds that require constant grooming to keep their coats looking good. One look at the Basset, and it's obvious that he is never going to need much in the way of haircuts and trims to keep him looking dapper and sharp. However, you should never neglect your Basset's grooming or consider it unimportant just because he won't ever need the in-depth grooming, trimming, and sculpting that some of his cousins require.

Bassets, like most other hound breeds, tend to develop body odor if they're not bathed regularly. However, you should always keep a close watch on both his teeth and ears when he starts emitting an odor. Do not assume that any smells are coming only from his skin. Many times, an odor can be a warning signal of a potential health problem instead of simply the need for a bath.

WASH AND WEAR DOGS?

The time you spend grooming your Basset isn't just a beautification ritual. It should be a time of bonding with him; checking his body for bruises, cuts, insect bites, or other injuries; and keeping an eye out for lumps, bumps, and other anomalies that can be deadly without early detection. Don't listen to the hype that Bassets are "wash and wear" dogs. While they don't require the hours of brushing time that their longer-haired cousins require, any good grooming session should be more than a cursory bath and quick brushing. Grooming is a chance to spend time with your Basset. Make sure he knows that grooming time is quality time, and that both of you enjoy it.

SKIN AND COAT CARE

Brushing

Far from being strictly a "wash and wear," drip-dry kind of dog, a Basset's smooth, short

coat and skin need regular attention. Although they don't have long flowing hair that requires daily brushing to eliminate mats and tangles, a Basset Hound still needs regular brushing—especially when he is shedding (which for some Bassets may seem like a year-round event).

You should brush your Basset once a week. Regular brushing will not only contribute to the health of the skin and coat, because it distributes the natural oils through the coat, but it will help diminish shedding problems.

Instead of the usual slicker or pin brushes used on coated breeds, a shedding blade, grooming mitt, or coarse washcloth will work wonders on your Basset's coat, keeping him glossy, shiny, and healthy looking. Using your grooming mitt or washcloth, start at the head and work your way back, brushing with the hair of your dog.

Your Basset's smooth, short coat and skin need regular attention.

Shedding

Bassets seem to shed more than some other breeds, but through proper grooming and nutrition, you can do a lot to keep down the amount of loose hair you'll find in your home and on your clothes. In addition to the need to pull out dead hair using a shedding blade or other shedding tool for short dense coats, you should always keep your Basset on a nutritionally sound diet. Shedding is controlled by hormonal changes that most researchers believe are tied to photoperiod (length of natural light in a day), as well as to the level of nutrition received on a regular basis and the dog's general state of health. All breeds go through a biennial shedding, and dogs may lose hair after being under anesthesia for X-rays or surgery, or after having puppies.

Brushing and rubbing your dog using the proper tools not only will help eliminate dead hair that would have eventually ended up on your carpet or wool blazer, but will keep his skin soft, supple, and healthy.

Skin Care

A dog cannot be considered "well groomed" unless he has healthy skin. Grooming is essential for healthy skin, not only for keeping it clean and massaging it to bring out the skin's natural oils, but for allowing you to check for any skin problems that may be developing. If you notice any anomalies of the skin during your grooming session, alert your veterinarian immediately. A dull coat combined with dry, itchy, or sore skin can be a symptom of disease. A malfunctioning thyroid, for example, can quickly take your Basset from being a poster boy to looking like a haggard stray.

BATH TIME

Many people who have Bassets claim that their dogs don't need frequent baths, while others say they have to bathe their dogs fairly often. It seems to be not only a matter of personal preference from owner to owner, but also a difference in need from dog to dog. The rule of thumb should be to only bathe your Basset when he is truly dirty or has body odor (remember to check teeth and ears and not assume that all odor comes from the body). Too-frequent baths can do more harm than good, because they can dry the skin's natural oils, which can lead to scratching, then bacterial infections and "hot spots." If you're a fastidious owner who insists on bathing your Basset more than once a month, be sure you use a shampoo that has aloe or other skin-conditioning ingredients, and follow up with a good skin-conditioning coat dressing.

Splish Splash, I Was Takin' a Bath...

It doesn't take a rocket scientist to bathe a dog, but having the right tools and some basic information can certainly make the job a lot easier. To make bath time a happy time for your Basset:

- *Place a rubber mat in the bottom of your tub.* A Basset who is slipping and sliding around the tub is going to be an unhappy dog who will do his best to escape his slippery torture chamber. The ability to keep his feet firmly planted in place will make him feel more secure and will allow him to stand

Where to Brush Your Basset

Most people seem to prefer getting down on the floor with their Basset and incorporating grooming time with petting and play time. Using a grooming table isn't really a good idea unless you have a ramp for the Basset to walk up to the table. Not only could you easily injure yourself trying to lift him up and down, but since Bassets are prone to spinal injuries, this can be an invitation to trouble for them as well.

Check for Fleas

You also should use your grooming time to look for external parasites that your dog may have picked up on a foray into the great outdoors. Many Bassets are prone to flea allergies, which not only can cause mild to severe discomfort, but can create a staphylococcus infection that can be quite difficult to eliminate. Finding the problem quickly (daily checks are imperative during flea season), getting rid of the fleas efficiently, and treating any resulting irritation or infection correctly can help keep your dog's skin and coat in perfect condition. Not only can flea allergies and the resulting infections be hard on your dog's skin and coat, but they also can do quite a bit of damage to your wallet, since the antibiotics necessary to combat infections of the skin are expensive.

Don't depend on your naked eye to find fleas when you're grooming. Use a fine-tooth comb or a flea comb made specifically for this purpose. If you don't find any live fleas, but are finding tiny black grains of dirt, your dog does indeed have fleas. The black specks aren't dirt (or eggs as some people believe) but are dried flea feces. If you moisten them, you'll see the redness as the dried blood in the feces becomes hydrated. If you're shampooing your dog, and the water has a pink tinge, that's the reason. You should either use a shampoo designed to kill fleas or follow a bath with a flea dip. Once the immediate problem has been taken care of, ask your vet what once-a-month flea preventative they suggest for your area. Remember, no dog who has fleas is going to have healthy skin, and unhealthy skin cannot grow a healthy coat.

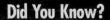

Did You Know?

You always should use lukewarm water in the bathing process, because hot water can shock the hair and cold water does not do as good a job of penetrating the hair shaft.

quietly as he's scrubbed.

- *Only use lukewarm water.* Not too hot, not too cold. In the summertime, you can likely get away with bathing your Basset outdoors using the hose, but don't attempt it in cooler weather. Not only will you make your Basset hate bath time, but you can possibly make him sick if he's unused to being cold and wet (and what proper Basset house dog would be?).

- *Have all your supplies within reach before you put the dog in the tub.* If you forget something and have to leave the room, be prepared to chase him down again. Only the most well-behaved Basset will sit in the tub patiently waiting for you to get your act together.

- *Place a cotton ball inside each ear (the Basset's, not yours), but not too far inside.* This will help keep water from draining into the ear canal—a cause of some ear infections.

- *Be sure you work the shampoo into a thick lather, and scrub every inch of your dog's body.* If he doesn't like having his face scrubbed, try doing that with a washcloth and baby "no tears" shampoo. If you're using a flea shampoo, wash the face first, then work your way to the dog's tail.

- *Use a shampoo that is formulated for your dog's skin.*

- *Be sure you rinse well.* Shampoo left in the hair and on the skin can cause an irritation. Cover your dog's eyes with your hand while you're rinsing to avoid getting shampoo spray in his eyes.
- *Use a rinse-out conditioner after the shampoo.* Even a tough Basset coat needs a moisturizer or conditioner during winter months, especially when hair shafts may become dry and brittle.

When you are finished, remove the cotton balls from his ears. Using your hands, squeegee the excess water from his body, legs, and tail. Dry his coat using old towels. In warm weather, your Basset can be allowed to air dry almost anywhere, but in cold weather, it's a good idea to place his crate near a heater or other warm air vent until he has dried. Hair dryers can be used, but be warned that most dogs must be trained to accept them. Always use the dryer on the coolest setting.

Your choice of shampoo is extremely important. Using harsh shampoos can dry out your dog's hair and create static electricity, but using a shampoo with too many moisturizers can actually oversoften his coat and make it appear limp, lifeless, and oily. Experiment with shampoos to find one that provides the best cleansing agents along with the proper amount of moisturizers and conditioners to keep your dog's coat texture as good looking as possible.

Never dry your dog with a human hair dryer, unless the dryer has a "cool" or "air only" setting. Dog hair (or human hair too for that matter) that has been exposed to too much heat will form gas bubbles in the hair shaft cavities, which is actually an early stage of combustion.

Some owners, especially those involved in dog shows, use a grooming table, but be sure to have a ramp for your Basset to climb up onto the table.

Prolonged exposure to this heat will leave your pet with kinky, brittle, and totally unmanageable hair as the result. The average human hair dryer produces air that is heated to about 300°F (149°C). Be very sure to keep the air vents unclogged in any hair dryer (for humans or animals) that you use, because a clogged air vent creates vastly hotter air than a dryer that has air moving freely through its vents—this can raise the temperature of the air to almost 600°F (315°C). A hair dryer that overheats will cause more than just a "bad hair day" and can cause skin injury to your Basset.

ANAL SAC CARE

Your Basset has small glands at about the eight o'clock and four o'clock positions on each side of the anus. The fluid contained in these sacs is extremely foul smelling. Many dog behaviorists and researchers agree that this odor provides the means of identification between individual animals (which explains why dogs go around sniffing each other there). Normally, these sacs empty with every bowel movement, and sometimes a pet will express his glands when he's scared, nervous, or upset. However, factors such as obesity, internal parasites, allergies, and low-fiber diets can lead to anal gland impaction.

Although it's probably the very least pleasant aspect of dog ownership, it's very important that you check your dog's anal glands regularly. If you see him scooting around on his rear end, it's very likely that an anal gland irritation or impaction exists. If left untreated, these glands can become infected quickly, which is not only very painful for the dog, but requires treatment that you both will likely find quite unpleasant.

Emptying the sacs is quite simple (although admittedly quite unpleasant for everyone involved). Simply place your thumb and index finger just below the anus, covering the anal opening with a tissue to catch the fluid. Squeeze gently, pressing inward and upward on the sacs simultaneously. This should cause the fluid within to be evacuated. Be prepared for a very oily, foul-smelling elimination that is not water-soluble and is therefore very hard to remove from clothes or skin. If you should have an accident, use isopropyl alcohol followed by soap and water to remove the odor. You can cover your dog's hindquarters with an old towel until you become somewhat adept at the procedure.

If you need assistance in learning how to express the anal

Bathing Tip

The most common mistake made when bathing a dog is not wetting the hair down thoroughly enough. Water is the dispersing agent for your shampoo—it distributes it and swells the hair shaft. This swelling helps open the cuticle to allow better penetration of the shampoo and conditioners. You should always wet the coat, wait for a couple of minutes for the water to absorb into the coat, and wet again.

glands, ask your veterinarian to show you how it's done. Be sure you know what you're doing before you attempt it, because using too much pressure can bruise the area, causing your dog a great deal of pain. If you decide not to do this yourself, your vet or a local groomer will do it for you for a nominal fee.

EAR CARE

The long, floppy ears of the Basset are not conductive to good air circulation, which makes them prone to painful and possibly severe ear infections. Keeping the ears clean as part of a regular grooming session can go a long way toward eliminating health problems that originate in the ear canal.

You should clean the inside of your Basset's ears once a week with a mild astringent or foaming ear cleanser (available from most pet supply stores or your veterinarian). Many good "recipes" also are available for making homemade ear washes, but always check with your veterinarian before using them on your pet. Some dogs have more sensitive ears than others, so it's a good idea to use any

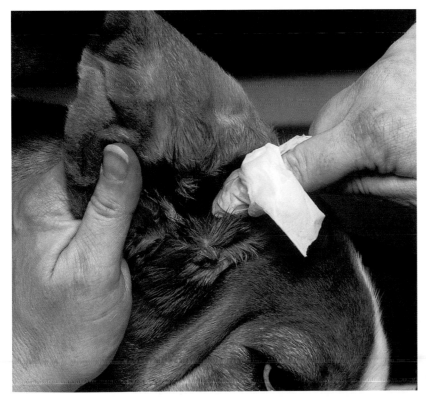

Keeping your Basset's ears clean as part of a regular grooming session can go a long way toward eliminating health problems that originate in the ear canal.

product with caution, even after getting a green light from your vet.

To use these cleaning solutions, apply liberally to the inside of the ear and massage gently, making sure the solution goes deep into the dog's ear. Then use a tissue, cotton ball, or baby wipe to clean away the residue. Don't use a swab—leave the deep cleaning of the ear with a swab to a professional, because you can injure the ear canal with deep probing. Be careful—as soon as you take your hand from his ear, the dog will likely shake his head, which can splash you with the dirty solution. Don't forget to wipe the outside of the ear flaps as well as the inside and the outer canal, since the ears will be dragged through dirt, puddles, food, and other nasties.

You should start cleaning a puppy's ears as soon as you bring him home, so that he'll get used to the treatment and learn to enjoy it. Ear cleaning is also good time to look for ear mites, fleas, and ticks. Ticks seem especially attracted to the folds of a Basset's ears, and smaller ones can hide quite easily, so be certain that you look carefully inside all the nooks and crannies.

EYE CARE

You should always check your dog's eyes as part of your grooming routine. With their droopy eyes and prominent haws (the third eyelid or membrane in the inside corner of the eye), the

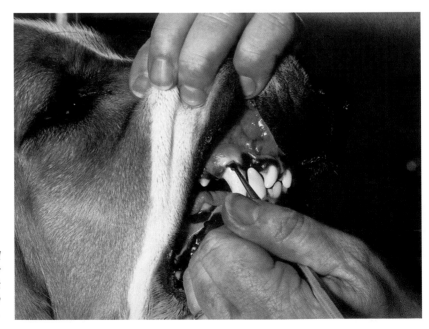

Your Basset's teeth need to be given proper attention—you can ask your vet for tips on how to take care of them.

Basset's eyes are prone to irritation. Unless an infection is present, you will not need to clean his eyes regularly. When you give your dog his bath, you can put mineral oil in his eyes. This will protect the eyes from any debris, loose hair, or shampoo that might get into them. While mineral oil can't be considered a cure for dry eye, it does lubricate the eye.

DENTAL CARE

Just as we visit our dentist regularly because we know the importance of good dental health, so should our dog's teeth be given proper attention. Human teeth are affected by dental caries, something unknown in the world of dogs. However, tartar is just as much an enemy to good canine dental hygiene as it is to that of a human. Tartar accumulates much more rapidly at the gum line in a dog's mouth than it does on a human tooth. If this tartar is allowed to continue to build up, it can create gum irritation, which can become an infection, which can ultimately affect a dog's entire health—compromising not only his healthy "smile," but also possibly contributing to serious heart conditions.

Visiting the Dentist

Regular visits to a canine dentist help keep your dog healthy and happy. Cleaning, polishing, and scaling their patient's teeth are as routine to canine dentists as they are to those of a human—and just as important. So is daily brushing and even flossing in some situations. Ask your veterinarian what she suggests for the continued good dental health for your dog.

It is important to realize the importance of good dental health for your dog. It's not just a matter of keeping down oral odors and keeping your dog's full set of teeth. Periodontal disease not only harms the teeth and gums, but severe cases involve bacterial toxins that are absorbed into the blood supply and can cause permanent, even fatal damage to the heart and kidneys. In lesser cases, symptoms of periodontal disease can include loose teeth, loss of appetite, bad smelling breath, and diarrhea and vomiting.

How to Brush Your Basset's Teeth

- Find a quiet time when you and your dog are relaxed and comfortable.
- Make sure to use a toothpaste formulated for pets, because some ingredients in human toothpaste can be harmful to your dog. Remember, he isn't able to spit it out after the brushing. Most dogs love the chicken-flavored toothpaste available at pet supermarkets.
- If his teeth have never been brushed before, don't try to use a toothbrush the first time. Just place a dab of toothpaste on your finger and let him taste it, then rub his teeth with your fingertips. This may take more than one attempt before he

realizes this is a pleasurable experience.

- After he is used to having your finger in his mouth, place a small amount of toothpaste on the brush. Using a slow, circular motion, brush one or two teeth and the adjoining gum line. Again, this may take a few tries before your dog accepts it easily.

- Over the next few days, gradually increase the number of teeth you brush until you are allowed to brush the rear teeth, where plaque and tartar buildup can do the most damage. You should eventually work up to brushing about 30 seconds per side. Don't worry about the inside surfaces, because dogs don't usually build up much tartar there. Just be certain you reach the outside surface of all the teeth, especially those rear ones.

- Stop each session while it is still fun for your dog, and don't spare the praise afterwards! He'll soon start looking forward to the time spent with you, and the special attention (as well as that great-tasting toothpaste).

Chewing for Dental Health

All dogs must be given the proper items to chew on during the various stages of their life. Bassets don't chew more than any other breed, but they can be destructive if they aren't given the proper chew toys.

Your Basset needs proper chew toys for the various stages of life.

Take Doggy Breath Seriously

No one likes to be around a dog with really bad breath. Although you can mask the odor with chew toys or charcoal biscuits, you should find the root cause of the odor. Although the bad odor may come from something nasty your pet has eaten or licked, it could be caused by something more serious.

The most common cause of halitosis is periodontal disease, which is caused by plaque (bacteria). Other causes include metabolic disease (diabetes, uremia); respiratory disease (rhinitis, sinusitis, neoplasia); gastrointestinal disease (megaesophagus, neoplasia, foreign bodies); dermatologic disease (lip fold pyoderma); or nonperiodontal oral disease (orthodontic, pharyngitis, tonsillitis, neoplasia).

As you can see, bad breath isn't just pesky, it can be a potential health threat. If you notice your Basset's breath smelling foul, have a veterinarian check him thoroughly. In the meantime, you can make your dog's breath fresher with this easy (and dogs say tasty) recipe to help neutralize the problem, using activated charcoal, which is readily available at your local pharmacy or market.

No-More-Bad-Breath Biscuits

2 cups brown rice flour

1 tablespoon activated charcoal

3 tablespoons canola oil or vegetable oil

1 egg

1/2 cup chopped fresh mint

1/2 cup chopped fresh parsley

2/3 cup low-fat milk

Preheat oven to 400°F (204°C). Combine the flour and activated charcoal in a small bowl. Add the rest of the ingredients, mixing well after each addition. Using a teaspoon, drop the biscuits about 1 inch (2.5 cm) apart onto a well-greased cookie sheet. Bake the biscuits for 15 to 20 minutes, or until golden brown. Cool thoroughly. Store the biscuits in the refrigerator in an airtight container.

Puppies and young dogs especially need something with resistance to chew on while their teeth and jaws are developing. This will help them cut their puppy teeth at the appropriate time, induce the growth of the permanent teeth already forming beneath those puppy teeth, and assist in getting rid of the puppy teeth when it's time for the permanent adult teeth to come through the gums. Keeping a puppy's teeth "on schedule" is very important, because it assures proper jaw development and makes certain that the permanent teeth are settled solidly in the jaws.

An adult dog also needs to chew. No, he won't be losing any teeth (hopefully), and he doesn't have more teeth waiting in the wings so to speak, but nature tells him how important it is to chew things for natural tooth cleaning, gum massage, and jaw exercise, to say nothing of releasing pent-up doggie tension. For some dogs, a proper chew toy can be a veritable pacifier to keep him satisfied when his human isn't around. Tooth and jaw development continue until a dog is well past his first birthday, it and can continue far longer if the dog's health has been compromised by injury or disease.

Because you don't want your puppy cutting his teeth on your new shoes, or your older dog chewing on something they could break or accidentally ingest, it's very important to provide adequate chew toys for your dog throughout his life—not just for entertainment, but for his general health. Be sure you choose items that will be long lasting, good tasting, entertaining, and completely safe from breaking or chipping. The best chew toys are natural bones, preferably something like 4- to 8-inch-long round shin bones. You can also try out bones made of nylon, like Nylabones, which can make long-lasting chews for your Basset.

Get your puppy used to having his nails trimmed as soon as you bring him home.

NAIL CARE

Although some dogs keep their nails worn down without help from you, most dogs need to have their nails trimmed on a regular basis. Nails that are not kept short will grow too long and become irritating and painful to the dog. A longer nail is much more prone to being pulled out if it catches on something, which can be excruciating for the dog. Being left too long can not only damage the nails, but can cause the feet to splay or spread, and nails can actually curl around and grow into a dog's pads.

Your dog's nails should just touch the ground when he walks. If his nails are clicking on the floor or getting snagged in the carpet, it's time for a pedicure. Although nail trimmers look like an instrument of torture, in the right hands, with a little bit of knowledge, they can be totally painless.

How to Trim Your Basset's Nails

The steps for correctly trimming your dog's nails are:

- Use nail trimmers designed for pets. You can ask your vet or groomer what type of trimmers they suggest. Most will suggest the guillotine type (which are not nearly as deadly as they sound).

- Make sure the clippers are sharp. Dull nail trimmers can split the nail instead of giving a nice sharp cut. This may cause the nail to split upwards into the quick, which can be quite painful for the dog.

- Look for the "quick"—the part of the nail that contains nerves and blood vessels. It is very painful and will bleed easily if cut. On white nails it shows up as pink, but is harder to see on darker nails.

- Start at the tip of the nail and snip a little at a time. When you come close to the quick (the part that is more than just a "shell"), stop.

- If you trim too short, and the nail begins to bleed, apply pressure, then dab with a styptic powder, baby powder, or white flour. Some people recommend using granulated sugar, or pressing your dog's bleeding nail into a soft bar of soap. Once the bleeding is stopped, be careful not to wipe the clot from the end of the nail.

- If your dog's dewclaws (the fifth claw on the inside of the leg) were not removed when he was a puppy, don't forget to trim them too. Since it never touches the ground, it grows faster, and can grow into a circle, eventually digging into your dog's skin and causing a potential health problem.

- Trim nails once or twice a month. The quick will lengthen if the nails are not trimmed often, so you won't be able to keep the nails as neat and tidy as you might like. Long nails can cause traction problems and may cause the foot shape to look improper.

Grooming Time as Bonding Time

Grooming your Basset accomplishes much more than simply making your pet's coat look nice and keeping him fresh smelling. It is a time of bonding— sharing quality time with your dog that you won't have with any other activity. Don't consider grooming him a chore, but rather something special you both should look forward to.

TRAINING *and* BEHAVIOR
of Your Basset Hound

here's an old chestnut that says before you can train a dog, you must know more than the dog. Although that usually garners a laugh from the crowd, it's actually quite true. Obviously, you are more intelligent than your dog—but before you can be a good trainer, you have to get inside a dog's mind and figure out how he thinks. Therefore, from a dog's point of view, to be able to teach him, you must know more than the dog and be the leader of his pack.

SOCIALIZATION: WHY IS IT IMPORTANT?

No matter what type of training you decide to pursue, socialization is a must for any dog. The socialization we receive as children teaches us how to interact appropriately with other humans throughout our lives. Humans need good social skills to be able to function in the workplace as well as the social scene. For this reason, our children are urged to learn to play nicely with other children, and they are entered into playgroups and preschool, where they learn to socialize according to the rules of our society.

It is just as important for our dogs to learn adequate canine social skills. A responsible dog owner will take the job of socializing their pet very seriously. It will be up to his human to teach a puppy the social skills he needs, during the very small window of opportunity given because of their rapid growth patterns. His mother will have taught him his "manners" when dealing with her and his siblings, but it is up to you to teach him how he should interact with other humans and the other animals he will come into contact with throughout his life.

Most animal behaviorists agree that the optimum opportunity for the socialization of a puppy occurs between the ages of 8 and 14 weeks. Socialization after that period, for a puppy who has not received adequate interaction with humans and other animals, will be a much longer and frustrating procedure. Not impossible, certainly, but a definite challenge.

No matter the puppy's or dog's age, the socialization procedure should be much the same.

To correctly socialize your puppy, you should:

Training Tip

If you decide to engage in organized sports, it will be necessary for you to get some expert training help, at least at the beginning. Joining a training class is a great way to meet other people who share your interest and will happily share their experience with you. You can hire a personal trainer to help with your homework, or join forces with someone from the club who will work with you as you learn how to teach your dog.

- Introduce your puppy to as many humans as possible: all ages, both sexes, and of many different races and cultures. Make these meetings positive and, if possible, have treats available for each new person to give to the puppy. This will keep your puppy from reacting negatively to someone he meets who doesn't look or sound exactly like his own family.
- Introduce him to children in a manner totally different from that which you use to introduce older adults. The puppy should learn not to jump up on them or play too hard with them, and the children should learn to respect the puppy's feelings accordingly. Before a dog can be "good with children," he must be exposed to children that are "good with dogs."
- Teach your puppy to allow humans to be near when he is eating. If you hand-feed your puppy for a few days, then set the bowl down and add your puppy's favorite treats to the dish as he eats them, he will quickly learn that having humans near his food bowl is a positive thing. If he reacts aggressively to any contact when he is eating, measures should be taken to the correct the behavior immediately, and you should contact a professional. Possessiveness of food can quickly escalate to being held hostage by a dog who doesn't "allow" humans to be near anything he considers his.
- Teach your puppy to greet visitors with all four feet on the floor. This usually can be accomplished if you ignore the puppy until he is calm. This means no eye contact, no physical contact, and if possible, completely ignoring him until he behaves.
- Expose your puppy to the noises he is likely to come in contact with throughout his life: loud cars, vacuum cleaner, hair dryer, dishwasher, lawnmower, radio, TV, and any other noise that might be startling if it occurs to an unsuspecting animal. Don't make a big issue of the noise. If he appears startled, do not cuddle him or tell him it is "all right." Doing so tells him it is "all right" to be upset, that it is indeed something about which he should be concerned. As soon as he shows a recovery from being startled, give him a treat and tell him how brave he was. To introduce your puppy to traffic noises, always make sure you have a firm hold on his leash, and start out on a slower street before you progress to a busier part of town. If you live in a rural area, introduce him only to animals you are certain

will not hurt him.

- Introduce your puppy to other animals carefully. Be certain they are not allowed to traumatize him, tease him, or hurt him. In turn, be sure that he is not allowed to terrorize, overwhelm, or harm the other animals. Most animals will quickly sort out their pecking order, and most will be tolerant of a puppy, but will give sharper corrections as the puppy gets older. Unless the puppy is likely to be actually harmed or severely traumatized by excessively strong discipline by his peers, allow them to work through the situation on their own.

- Make sure your puppy learns to spend time alone happily. A puppy who is never alone will become a dog who will likely suffer separation anxiety and become overly stressed as soon as his owner goes out of sight. Even if your puppy whines pitifully when he is left alone, be strong. Give him a fun toy to play with in his crate or sleeping area, and walk out of sight. Stay away until he settles down and plays quietly by himself. Then come back into the room, praise him, and give him a treat.

Make sure you socialize your Basset with other pets.

Remember that it takes proper socialization to become the companion that we all expect our dogs to be. It is our responsibility to provide our dogs with the opportunity to learn the things they need to know to become good members of our society.

Puppy Kindergarten

Puppy kindergarten is a great way to help socialize your Basset—he'll learn to interact with other humans and dogs. Your veterinarian or local kennel club can give you information about any puppy kindergarten classes in your area. Puppy classes consist of some basic obedience training as well as socialization. It also gives a professional a chance to watch how you interact with your dog and give you pointers that can help you avoid problems down the road.

Puppy kindergarten is not only necessary for your puppy to learn to socialize with other dogs and humans, but it's a place for the two of you to develop a closer relationship. A well-run puppy kindergarten should teach you how to teach your puppy. The instructor should have a gentle voice, and your puppy will likely think she's quite wonderful. Working together, you will teach your puppy basic commands such as sit, stay, come, down, and heel.

It's important to realize that, as with any type of schooling, doing your homework will definitely improve your final grade (the difference between growing up into a well-trained adult versus an ill-trained hellion). Remember to keep your training sessions at home short and full of fun. End them on a positive note, with a well-earned treat. A puppy's attention span is short, and any distractions will draw his attention away from the job at hand. Keeping the lessons short and fun will go a long way toward making him enjoy them and, in the end, he'll learn more. Although the lessons should be short, you can have several during the day. Incorporate learning experiences into games and other play times, so your dog is learning even when he doesn't know it.

Treating Problem Behaviors

Problem behaviors are much more easily dealt with as they start, rather than waiting until they are deeply ingrained. A canine professional can spot potential problems and show you how to deal with them to help make your puppy grow up into a responsible member of your family.

THE BASICS: UNDERSTANDING AND SETTING RULES

One of the most important things you can do for your Basset is to teach him early on that you are the leader in his pack. Ground rules must be laid at the start of the relationship, and you must not vary from them. What you don't consider acceptable behavior in an adult shouldn't be allowed in a puppy. While you may think it's cute to hear your puppy growling as you play, and you don't find his playful nips painful, in an older dog, these actions can become dangerous. Don't allow this behavior in the beginning, and it won't become a problem later. The same is true for other house rules. If you don't plan on allowing your pet on the furniture at any time, be firm with this rule, even when he's a cute, cuddly puppy. If you're not going to accept the behavior later, don't allow it at all.

Although your dog may complain when he's reminded of his status, believe me, you're doing him a favor. A dog is happiest when he knows what his lot is in life. He likes knowing who his leader is and what it takes to keep you happy. He will be happiest when he knows what is expected of him, and exactly what limits have been set as acceptable behavior.

Let Basset Be Basset

To truly enjoy your Basset, you must let him be a Basset. What is acceptable behavior for a human isn't acceptable for a dog, and vice versa. Dogs have evolved into the different breeds we know today through select discrimination and selective breeding. You should understand what is proper Basset behavior before you attempt to change something you may find unacceptable, but is

Puppy kindergarten can help your puppy learn to socialize with other dogs.

indeed a part of a Basset's true and inherent character. Be aware of what makes a Basset a Basset, and learn to love the foibles that make this a unique breed: Exasperating at times—but all who love this breed say that the problems are far outweighed by the joy that these flop-eared clowns bring into their life.

Their happy, effervescent character belies the Basset's history as a serious hunting dog. These lovable clowns have an irrepressible joy of life and, in turn, bring joy to those around them. Their history ties in with their character in other ways, however—as gun dogs, to be truly worthy of their title, they must be highly intelligent and readily trainable, and must have an aggressive, yet steady, temperament. The Basset Hound is indeed a very intelligent creature; intelligent enough to worm his way to the position of pack leader if he is owned by someone who doesn't have the knowledge and understanding to gain his respect and become the leader.

TYPES OF TRAINING

Dog training can be accomplished at many different levels. Most people are happy to train their dog to be a responsible family member and then just maintain the basics as time goes by. Equipped with a good training book and a desire to make their Basset truly part of the family, almost anyone can manage this type of training.

Other owners want to train their dogs to do tricks or some simple chores (fetch the newspaper, slippers, or his leash when he wants to take a walk). Armed with a good book on training, and a dog who has a desire to please, this is an easily attainable goal as well.

Others train their dogs to actually work for them: hunting, tracking, search and rescue, therapy, guiding, or other jobs suited to their breed. This requires a lot more on the part of the trainer, and it will likely be necessary to get the support of a professional in whatever avenue you choose to focus your attention. It will also require that your dog have the desire to do the job. A dog who is asked to do something he really does not enjoy will soon burn out, and training will become a chore instead of a pleasure for you both. While some Bassets were born to hunt, others enjoy tracking (either as a competitive sport, as part of search-and-rescue teams, or both). Still others find their niche in the world as therapy dogs, bringing smiles to the faces of sick children or the residents of nursing homes.

Be a Good Leader

Your Basset should not fear you, but he must always respect you and know that you are the leader, not him.

Still other owners find the rapport they get with their dog while training so interesting and fulfilling that they continue to work diligently with their dog to ready him for ongoing competition in obedience, agility, flyball, and other competitive dog sports. While Bassets aren't the fastest dogs in the lineup, and you likely won't get top scores with them in timed sports when pitted against faster breeds (and their stubborn nature makes it a challenge to compete in obedience), these sports are great exercise for them and many owners enjoy the challenge.

Keep It Fun and Positive

Whether you want your dog simply to be able to realize what you expect from him (basic training), want him to work with you (hunting, tracking, search and rescue), or become competitive at canine events, you will find the time spent together a bonding and wonderful experience. Just remember, until he is sure of what you want him to do, you must exhibit special patience with him. If your temper starts getting frayed, it is time to walk away and never let him know that he's upset you. Remember, being a leader means exhibiting the kind of behavior you expect from your subordinates.

Bassets don't take kindly to scolding or harsh training. They also bore easily and can become stubborn if they are repeatedly asked to do something they don't understand. Keep your lessons short and interesting, and make sure that he knows exactly what you're asking him to do. Use lots of positive reinforcement. Keep in mind that the way to a Basset's mind is through his tummy. Keep a pocket full of his favorite treats whenever you are going to attempt to teach him anything new, and always end each training session on a positive note when he has done something correctly.

Make training a positive experience for your Basset to keep him interested and motivated.

HOUSETRAINING AND CRATE TRAINING

Crate training and housetraining go hand in hand. It is certainly much easier and faster to housetrain a dog if you use a crate.

Dogs are den animals. In the wild, den animals do not urinate or

How Long Can My Basset Stay in the Crate?

Remember that you should never keep a dog in a crate longer than his bowel and bladder can manage. Puppies have very tiny bladders, and their sphincter muscles are too undeveloped to hold waste for long periods of time. Except during the night, when they should be sleeping, two hours is usually an acceptable length of time to keep your Basset in the crate. Keeping a puppy or an adult confined to a crate for long periods is cruel, not only because he was not meant to be alone for so long, but his bowel and bladder can be damaged from trying to "hold it" for too long. Your Basset will be much more prone to bladder stones if he is not allowed to empty his bladder on a reasonable schedule. Sooner or later, a dog kept confined in a crate for too long at a time will begin eliminating in his crate; once that habit is ingrained, remedial crate training will be a long, uphill battle.

defecate near the place where they sleep. They will go as far as possible from their den to eliminate, so the scent does not attract predators to their home. You can take advantage of this inherent behavior by giving your Basset a crate as his very own "den." He will be reluctant to soil his den, and so you can use it to help you both get on a schedule for potty breaks.

A crate should never be used as a punishment, and your Basset should not be left in his crate for extended hours of time. Used properly, a crate is the most important tool a dog owner has. It becomes a mobile dog house—your dog's "special place" that he knows he can go to get away from the rest of the world. If you have children, make sure they understand that when he is in his crate, he is not to be disturbed.

How to Crate Train

When you're first introducing your puppy to a crate, leave the door open so that he can explore on his own. Never just push him inside, lock the door, and walk away. This will instill a fear of his crate as some sort of "prison."

Throughout the day, drop special treats inside the crate for him to find when he's exploring. After a while, you can get his attention and drop a biscuit in the crate and turn it into a game ("where's the cookie?"). When he finds it, praise him and let him know he did a wonderful thing by going into the crate when he was told (even though he just thought he was playing a game).

Then you can start closing the door for short periods of time, always making sure he has interesting toys to play with or a treat to eat. Make his crate a pleasant place by giving him a nice soft blanket, a newspaper area at the front (in case of accidents) and, in warm weather especially, a hamster-type water bottle that attaches to the outside of the crate. Once he's comfortable with being in his crate with the door closed (ignore him if he cries—don't comfort or scold him), you can start leaving him for short periods of time. Make the time longer and longer, until he no longer frets when he sees you leave.

Teaching your dog to be unafraid of being crated will make him much more welcome at the veterinarian's office, groomer, and boarding kennel, and will make it much easier to take him with you when you travel.

Housetraining takes patience and consistency.

How to Housetrain

All dogs have certain patterns that they follow throughout their lifetimes regarding their toilet practices. Once you understand those patterns, you can more effectively allow your dog the chance to eliminate when he needs to. Puppies must be given an opportunity to go to the bathroom immediately after they eat, as soon as they wake up, during their play times, first thing in the morning, and last thing at night. Young puppies need to eliminate every couple of hours; older puppies can go up to four hours between outside trips, and adults can go even longer (although they will certainly be happier and healthier if they are given more frequent opportunities).

When you take your dog outside for potty breaks, use the same command each time to remind him that he's there to tend to business and not play. Whether it's a code word that only you two know, or the more common "go potty" or "go outside," soon those words will be a trigger to your dog.

Once he's eliminated in the chosen place (whether it's outside or on newspapers), always give him a reward and praise him effusively. Let him know that you are absolutely thrilled with his actions. Don't rush him back inside as soon as he finishes his job. Take him for a walk, or play a game of catch with him. Spend some time with him before you go back inside.

Until your puppy is housetrained, confine him to a crate at night. No matter how pitiful he sounds, or how much it's bothering you, do not give in to his crying and whining. Buy earplugs if you have to, but don't make any contact with him so long as he is being vocal. Even scolding him is not acceptable—negative attention is still attention. That's what his crying and whining and carrying on is for—to get attention.

Before you crate him for the night, take him outside. Then wake up as early as possible to take him outside again. If you wake during the middle of the night, you can take him outside then, but don't spend time playing with him. Allow him a chance to use the bathroom, then put him back in his crate and leave him. Don't give in to his pitiful wailings.

In housetraining, as in all other aspects of training, patience is the key. If you use a crate responsibly, put your dog on a good feeding and walking schedule, learn to recognize his signals, and clean up thoroughly after every accident, most professional trainers

Accidents Happen

Under no circumstances should you rub your dog's nose in his excrement or urine. This is cruel, ineffective, and can backfire on you by making the dog more acceptable of the smell of his fecal matter and urine.

say you should be able to consider your puppy housetrained after 2 to 3 weeks. However, don't let down your guard once you think the job is completed. Even the best housetrained puppy or dog will fall into bad habits if you relax on his feeding schedule or exercise routines. Housetraining a dog requires commitment on your part, but the more consistent you are in following the basic housetraining procedures, the faster it will go.

Accidents

If your dog chooses your bed or furniture for his inside indiscretions, make those areas uncomfortable for him. This can be done by laying newspapers or inexpensive flannel backed vinyl tablecloths on the bed or furniture. Special mats also are created for this use; these mats set off a sonar sound when they're touched, which dogs find uncomfortable.

It's a common mistake for owners to take their dog outside, let him eliminate, then rush him back indoors. Unless your dog is begging to go back into the house for some reason, chances are that he will prefer spending some time out in the fresh air. Rushing him back inside quickly gives him the message that as soon as he eliminates his outside time will be over. Therefore, he takes as long as possible to do his business. Often, the owner will see this as a sign that the dog doesn't really have to go to the bathroom. So, inside they go, and the dog almost immediately pees or poops on the floor.

If your Basset has frequent accidents indoors, have your veterinarian check him to rule out any potential medical causes.

If your Basset doesn't eliminate on a trip outside, even after adequate time, take him inside, spend a little time with him, and then take him outside again.

Never punish your dog for accidents made in the house. Although sometimes they will seem to have been done in spite, this is not the case. The smartest dog in the world has the mentality of a very young child, and we all know that even older children have toilet accidents from time to time. We can certainly expect no less from our pets. If you catch your dog in the act of eliminating in the house, you should say sharply "no, no" or "outside" and quickly pick him up and take him outside.

It's very important that you supervise your unhousetrained dog at all times when he is indoors. This can be done with the judicious use of baby gates to confine your dog to a certain area. If your home is of open design, with not enough doorways to make gates an acceptable choice, you can put him on a leash that's attached to your belt. This keeps him near you, and you can easily watch for signals that he needs to take a trip outside.

It's important that you learn to recognize your dog's signals that he needs to go outside. Some signs are obvious—whining, walking to the door, looking at the doorknob longingly. Others may circle a few times and look distressed. Still others will have more subtle signals that you may have to learn through careful observation. Once you've learned his signal, never ignore it. And if you do, and an accident occurs, you should apologize to your dog and realize that maybe the problem in his housetraining isn't him, but you.

A harness might help you teach your Basset to walk nicely beside you.

Cleaning Up Accidents

The one sure thing about housetraining your dog is that you will be cleaning up a lot of accidents until he finally gets the message. It's vitally important that you completely and thoroughly clean up after every accident, to avoid repeat occurrences when the smell triggers your dog to make the same mistake again. As long as your pet can smell his personal "mark" in that area, he will continue to return to the scene of the crime.

How do you know exactly where the problem spots can be found? If you can't see it with your naked eye, purchase a black light bulb. Turn out all other lights, and the soiled areas will quickly pop into view. Before you turn the regular lights back on, outline the area with nonstaining chalk to be sure you treat the correct area.

When carpets get soiled by pets, the first thing that crosses some people's mind is to rent a steam cleaner, but nothing could be worse for preventing future accidents. Heat permanently sets the odor by bonding the protein into any man-made fibers. Also, putting vinegar or ammonia on the stain can actually enhance the odor to your Basset and make it more attractive to him.

It's very important to clean the area as soon as it is soiled. Use a combination of newspaper and paper towels to soak up urine. The more you can remove before it dries, especially from carpeting, the easier it will be to remove the odor. As soon as you discover a spot, place a few layers of paper towels on the wet spot, then cover that with a few layers of newspaper (putting newspaper directly on the spot can cause a stain from the newsprint). Step on the pile of papers and stand there for a moment, allowing your weight to press the paper into carpeting and draw the liquid up from the padding. Remove all layers of paper and repeat until the paper towel no longer picks up any dampness. Using cool water, rinse the area of the accident as well as possible, either picking up the water using the paper towel and newspaper padding effect, or using a vacuum cleaner designed to pick up water.

If your pet has soiled a washable item, you can wash it in your washing machine, adding baking soda to the wash cycle. Air drying the items reduces the chance that heat will set in any lingering odors. Also, adding an enzymatic cleaner to the wash cycle will help reduce any odors and bacteria.

When you clean your carpets, don't use any chemicals in the

Crate Tip

Make sure his crate is not too big, or he may be tempted to eliminate in a corner of the crate. Also, it's not a good idea to allow him any food or water before bedtime.

water; instead use an enzymatic cleaner designed to break down the protein of pet stains. Once your carpets are well cleaned, use a high-quality pet odor eliminator or neutralizer. Your veterinarian or other dog professional should be able to tell you what products work best for them.

When Accidents Mean Something Else

If, even after your best efforts, your dog continues to have accidents in the house, you should look into what might be the root of the problem.

You should have your puppy or adult checked out thoroughly by a veterinarian to rule out any medical reasons for the problems. A urinary tract infection or internal parasites will make it almost impossible for a dog to control his bladder or bowels. Both problems are usually fixed quite easily, and then you can begin housetraining again. A dog who has always been trustworthy in the house but suddenly begins having accidents should definitely see his veterinarian to rule out any illnesses or disease.

Some dogs temporarily lose control of their bladders if they become afraid or excited. They should never be scolded when this occurs, because this will only exacerbate the problem and their feelings of anxiety and fear.

An unneutered adult male will often "mark" his territory by sprinkling small amounts of urine throughout it. This usually can be stopped by having him neutered, although it will take time for his hormones to settle down enough to see a real difference in his behavior. Sometimes, males and females will mark their territory through urine or fecal deposits when their territory has been invaded by a newcomer. This is very common when a new pet, or sometimes even a new human baby, is introduced into the household.

Some dogs become so anxious at being left alone in the house that they will lose control of their bladder and bowels. This separation anxiety can be treated either with proper training or with the use of veterinarian-prescribed anti-anxiety medications. These medications also can be of use for dogs who have an inordinate fear of thunderstorms, fireworks, gunfire, or other loud noises. Some dogs have such an ingrained fear that, at the first sounds, they lose control of their bladder or bowels.

LEASH TRAINING

As soon as your Basset is a few months old, a leash will be necessary anytime he is outdoors and outside his fenced area. One of the most necessary things you will teach your dog is how to walk calmly on a leash, something that will be necessary throughout his life. Making sure he knows how to behave while being led will make things easier on both of you.

If he fights having the leash and collar put on him, allow him time to get used to them before attempting to take a walk. Put on the collar first and let him scratch it and worry and fret over it for a few minutes. Give him a treat to take his mind off it, and in a few minutes his attention will turn to something else, and the collar will become "old hat" to him. Later, attach the leash to it and allow him to drag it around (but watch that he doesn't catch it on anything). Then you can pick up the end and put a slight resistance on it. For a while, follow him wherever he goes, always with a slight resistance on the leash, so that he knows you are attached to

The nylon collar and leash this puppy is wearing are durable, washable, and come in many colors.

Trainers Training You

If you want to make sure you are doing the job correctly, you may want to hire a dog trainer to supervise your training methods and make suggestions—training you to train your dog, as it were. Most local kennel clubs offer basic training classes as well as classes for more involved training. Almost any veterinarian, groomer, pet sitter, or other dog professional will be able to point you in the direction of a good trainer. If you see someone with a very well-behaved dog, ask them how they achieved it. Check for flyers on the bulletin boards at veterinarians, farm supply stores, pet supply stores, and other pet-related markets. You also can check out the Association of Pet Dog Trainers (www.apdt.com) for recommended trainers in your area.

Be sure that the trainer you choose doesn't try to talk you into believing that harsh training methods will work better for your dog than any other. Positive reinforcement is the only training method that will work with a Basset. If they are bored or upset by the training, their stubborn nature will cause them to set their heels and refuse to learn. You must make it fun and make them want to do what you ask of them. A good trainer will know this, and she will work with you to make your dog the best that he can be.

him. Once he's used to that, call him to you and have treats when he comes. If he doesn't come, pull slightly to get his attention. Walk away from him, calling and offering a treat. Praise him when he walks where you want him to go.

Never pull the puppy along the floor by his collar. This can create lifetime problems of fear or anxiety. With patience, he'll learn that the slight resistance isn't a bad thing, and with the promise of treats, he'll happily walk alongside you. Always end your training session while he's walking happily. Praise him thoroughly and give him a treat.

Before you start walking with your dog on a leash, teach him to be calm while you're putting on the collar and leash. Don't allow it to become a puppy rodeo as you struggle to get a collar buckled and leash snapped into place. Make sure he learns that, if he's not calm enough to let you get the job done, he won't get to go for a walk at all.

Once he learns to be calm while he's being readied for the walk, it's time to teach him that once the collar is in place, it's not rodeo time again. If your dog drags you to the door and then down the street, things are out of control, and it's time for you to take control and be the leader. If your dog begins out-of-control behavior while on lead, simply stand still and gather up his leash until he runs out of slack. Say "no" or "settle down," and don't move until he stands quietly at your side. Then begin walking. If he starts pulling again, repeat the above. Do so as many times as it takes for him to begin walking calmly at your side. You can then give him a few inches at a time of leash so he can move farther away from you. Each time he gets unruly, stop and wait for him to come back to you, until he learns that if he wants to walk it has to be on your terms, not his. Remember, every time he lunges or pulls, and you continue walking, you are rewarding him for bad behavior. It is essential that you stand still and refuse to move until he is behaving. This may mean you don't cover much ground on your walks, but in time his little light bulb will go off, and he'll realize that if he walks calmly, he gets to see more territory. Again, patience pays off.

Choosing the Proper Collar and Leash

It's overwhelming to walk into a well-stocked pet store and see the array of leashes and collars available. Not only are a vast number of types and varieties available, but also an astounding display of colors, materials, and sizes. While some dogs will be able to go through their entire lives with only one type of leash and collar, most dogs will benefit from having an assortment of collars and leashes for whatever "job" they are involved in at the moment.

Collars

The most important thing about choosing a collar for your dog is getting one of the proper size. If your dog is going to be allowed outdoors unsupervised, in a fenced area, you should consider getting a collar with an "easy release" buckle in case he gets tangled in something. For outdoor use especially, even if your dog is microchipped, he should have an identification tag that has your name, address, and phone number attached to the collar. Although most rescue groups, shelters, and veterinarians can read microchip implants, having a contact name and phone number attached to him could get him returned to you much faster.

For your dog to be safe and comfortable, follow this rule of

Make sure you keep your training sessions short and fun – before you or your Basset tire out.

thumb (or rather, fingers) when ensuring a proper fit for his collar. Place two fingers between the dog's neck and the collar. There should be no more and no less room than the width of those two fingers. Too much space, and the collar can easily slip over the dog's ears. Too little space, and the dog will be uncomfortable. You should check occasionally to make sure the collar still fits correctly, because weight gain, or even thickening hair can cause the collar to become uncomfortable and even rub the skin raw.

Types of Collars
- *Buckle:* Buckle collars seem to be the overall choice for most dogs. Puppies especially should wear only buckle collars or harnesses to avoid accidental injury or choking. Most have a snap buckle, sometimes of plastic instead of metal. This is a good choice for a dog who gets wet often, because plastic won't rust like some metals, especially if the protective coating

over the metal gets scratched. Buckle collars come in a wide variety of materials (leather, vinyl, nylon) and colors. Many manufacturers now create "fashion statement" collars (some with matching leashes) that express the political views of the owner, sports team choices, or scenes of the season. Most adult Bassets will wear approximately a 20-inch (50 cm) collar, although the size may vary somewhat.

- *Choke Collars:* So named because they were designed to "choke" the dog who pulls too hard on the leash, these collars should only be used by a professional. They come in both nylon rolled cord, flat nylon, and chain, as well as "pinch" collars that have special links that have prongs that stick into a dog's neck if he misbehaves. Pinch collars can cause permanent damage to a dog if used incorrectly, and may cause injury or strangulation if the collar gets caught on something while the dog is left unattended. There should be no reason to use this type of collar on your Basset.

- *Martingale:* Also known as a "loop on loop" or "safety" collars, martingale collars were originally designed for dogs whose necks are larger than their heads (like Greyhounds and Whippets). They prevent the dog from escaping by self-tightening if the dog tries to back out. Many show leads used by conformation exhibitors are a combination of a type of martingale collar and a short leash.

Types of Collar Materials

- Nylon collars are durable, washable, and come in many colors, including prints. Nylon also can be embroidered, so you can have your dog's name or your phone number embroidered directly onto his collar. Nylon collars can be made from material that is either rope shaped or flat.

- Leather is as durable as nylon, but it doesn't come in the varied colors that nylon does. Leather wears well, however, and will soften from the oils in a dog's coat. Rolled leather collars (rolled into a tight round roll instead of lying flat) will not make the indention on your dog's coat as quickly or as indelibly as nylon; nor will it create static electricity in the coat as it rubs. Be aware that new leather can sometimes stain white hairs if it gets wet.

Harness

A dog harness will vary in appearance depending on the type, from those designed to provide assistance to the disabled, to those designed for training, for walking with a dog who insists on trying to pull his owner, or for a dog prone to disc injury. Some harnesses loop around the neck and body, some have a loop around the neck and a loop for both front legs, and some have an extra strap that goes over the nose for added control.

A harness keeps a dog from being able to pull as hard as he can with a normal collar, and may be recommended if your Basset tends to try to play "sled dog" with you when you're out on walks. You will have more control over him using a harness than you will using a traditional buckle collar, and your dog will be less likely to get a "whiplash" type injury that can occur with excessive tugging on a collar that goes only around his neck.

There's also a type of harness on the market made for dogs with arthritis, broken bones, or any other skeletal disorder that makes walking uncomfortable. The harness fits around the back legs, providing a support under the hips of the dog. The dog walker can lift slightly and eliminate stress on the back legs. The dog is still getting exercise, but some of the discomfort he experiences from

Treats are a great motivator for dogs, especially Bassets.

walking normally will be released as a portion of the weight is taken away.

Leashes

Leashes are measured by the length as well as the width or circumference of the material. For city walking, training to heel, or show in conformation, a shorter leash is usually better. For some training exercises and long leisurely walks, a longer leash is suggested. For teaching your dog to come when he is called, most trainers insist on a 6-foot (1.8m) cotton leash.

Types of Leashes

There are as many different types of leash as there are types of collars. Available in the same materials as collars—chain, leather, and nylon—the type of leash you choose depends on what you will be doing with your dog while he is on lead. Most people choose a leash that will match or complement their dog's collar.

- *Leather or nylon.* These are the most popular types of leashes, and either one would be fine to use on your Basset.
- *Chain.* Although chain leashes are still available, they are not recommended. Nylon or leather can both be just as sturdy, and you don't have the annoying clank of chain links to mar your quiet leisurely walks. Leather or nylon leashes also are easier on your hands.
- *Retractable.* If your dog spends a lot of time on a leash, you should consider purchasing a retractable leash. The nylon lead (some models have a nylon cord, others a flat nylon ribbon) is rolled up and housed in a plastic casing with a grip that you hold in your hand. Much like a fishing reel, a spring-type function doles out the lead as your dog pulls, and then retracts when the pressure is released. You can use the brake function of the leash to "reel" your dog in if he needs to be controlled.
- *Hands-free.* Hands-free leashes are available for joggers and bikers who want to enjoy their sport with their dog, without the hassle of handling the leash. These leashes attach to the human's waist and allows the owner to keep her hands free.
- *Bicycle leash.* The avid bicyclist can purchase a special bicyclist leash attachment for their bicycle that attaches from the bike's rear wheel to the dog's collar. This keeps your dog at a safe distance from your bicycle wheels, but allows him to

Tip When Teaching Come

A common mistake many owners make is to call their dog to come and then scold them for some transgression. Since a dog's memory isn't exactly Mensa quality, all the dog will remember is that he came to you and was scolded for it. Therefore, the next time you call, it's likely he won't come.

comfortably run alongside you. Because the lead is mounted below the center of gravity, it makes it almost impossible for your dog to be able to topple your bicycle.

- *Tie-out.* If you travel, or spend a lot of time camping or hiking, you should consider training your dog to stay happily on a tie-out leash. This is a long leash attached to a stake that is placed in the ground. The dog can move about, but is restricted to a specific area. Don't leave your dog unattended while he is on a tie-out leash, because he can become entangled and hurt himself.

BASIC COMMANDS

These commands are part of overall obedience training. With these basics, your dog will be much more easily controlled, and he will be happier because he knows he is doing exactly what you ask.

No matter what command you are teaching your dog, always end on a positive note. And decide on a phrase to use when the training exercise has finished, so that he knows it's play time. Remember that a Basset Hound is very food oriented, so keep a pocketful of treats to entice him to do his best during each training session. Remember to keep things fun. A Basset is easily bored, and if the training begins to feel like work, he'll set his heels and refuse to cooperate. And, as any dog trainer will tell you, trying to train a Basset who has decided he doesn't want to be trained is an exercise in futility.

Sit

This is usually one of the easiest commands to teach, so many owners start with it. The command "sit" is the basis of all obedience. All other commands will branch out from this one, making it the most important of all the training you do with your dog. Even if he learns no other command, learning to sit on command is of primary importance. When he is excited about going for a walk, and you can't put on his leash, tell him to sit and he's instantly in position. When you're out on a walk, and he sees a friend and wants to jump up on them, tell him to sit, and he's sure to get an extra pat from the friend. When he's nervous, telling him to sit gives him a chance to calm down, by doing something familiar and something he is confident he can do. Remember to always praise him when he properly responds to any command.

To teach sit, start with a treat in your hand. Raise it above your Basset's head, which will automatically cause him to sit. Say, "Sit," then treat and praise him as soon as he is in the sitting position. Repeat a few times a day, and soon he'll get the hang of it.

Down

The down position is usually one of the toughest to teach a dog. The down command is very important, especially if your Basset will be around small children. Lying down will put the dog on the child's level and make him seem less scary. Down is a submissive posture, which can make him seem less threatening to other dogs, possibly avoiding an altercation.

To teach down, start with your dog sitting. Say, "Down," and hold a treat in front of his nose. Slowly lower it to the ground, and treat and praise him when his elbows hit the ground.

Stay

Put your dog in the sit or down position, and with your hand out, palm facing your dog, say, "Stay." Then step right in front of him. Stay there. If he moves, say, "No" and put him back into position. When your dog will stay in place for 30 seconds, praise him (giving him treats or petting him will likely cause him to break

Teaching your Basset to always come when called can save his life in a dangerous situation.

the stay). Once your dog will stay in position with you right in front of him, begin taking a couple of steps away, until you are at the end of your 6-foot (1.8 m) leash. Once he masters this, you can begin walking out of sight (if you are indoors or another securely enclosed area). If he breaks from position, say, "No" and put him back into position. Eventually, your dog should learn to stay in whatever position he is told, even with distractions, until he is told that he can move.

Come

The come command may be the most important one you teach your puppy. Not only can it save his life by calling him away from danger, it can also help recall him in case he is lost and frightened.

Most behavioral problems can be resolved, but some may require help from a trainer or behavior consultant.

To teach the come command, put your puppy on a very long lead. Have a pocketful of his favorite treats. More just a few steps away from him, kneel down, and call in a happy voice, "Puppy come" (call him by name). Make sure that you call him in an excited and happy tone of voice. Dogs hear more how you say something than what you say, so you want him to be happy about coming toward you. Treat and praise him when he reaches you.

Continue to take him outside on his long leash and practice this command. If he becomes interested in something else, pull gently on the leash toward you, praising him as he comes. Continue to do this until he is fairly consistent about coming when he's called, then try the exercise off leash (always inside a fenced enclosure, of course).

Heel

Heeling is used for dogs shown in both conformation and obedience events. A heeling dog walks obediently next to the handler's left side. To teach this command, use a short leash on your dog, and say, "Heel" as you walk. Pull him into position so that his head is level with your leg as you are walking. Keep his leash pulled short, and keep him beside you as you continue to give the command. If he lunges ahead or lags behind, you should gently pull him into position.

PROBLEM BEHAVIORS

If your Basset is exhibiting problem behaviors, you should first establish that they are not the result of a health issue. A dog who suddenly forgets his housetraining may be suffering from a bladder or kidney infection or disease. A dog who suddenly becomes fearful or aggressive may have a problem that makes him hurt to be touched, or he may be losing his eyesight or hearing and is simply startled by things that would not faze a hearing or seeing dog. Take your dog to your veterinarian and explain the problems. Have her do a thorough checkup to be sure that some underlying medical problem isn't the culprit.

Often, excessive barking may be a sign of boredom or loneliness.

As soon as you know your dog is healthy and the behavior problem is just that—a problem rooted in his behavior—it's time to find a way to fix the problem. As a responsible pet owner, the thought of getting rid of your dog because he has a behavior problem should only be a last resort. Most problems can be worked on as long as you are properly armed with facts, professional help, dedication, and commitment. The goal is to get rid of the problem behavior, not the dog.

Finding a Behavior Consultant

If you find that your Basset's problems are greater than you can deal with on your own, you should look for a behavior consultant. He can help you come up with a game plan to work on the problem. How can you find the right person to work with you and your dog? You can ask your veterinarian or other pet professional (groomer, breeder, pet sitter) if they can recommend any behavior consultants or trainers in your area. Call around and find one who meets your needs and has a personality you think you can work with.

You should ask several questions of anyone you are considering as a potential trainer or consultant for your pet:

- Where and how long will the appointments be? Sixty to 90 minutes is usual for appointments.
- Who must attend? Make sure everyone involved in the problem and correction procedures can attend. If the dog is having problems with specific family members, or one particular "type" of person (male, female, person of other ethnic background, or people of a specific age group), it will be beneficial if that person can attend with you and your dog.
- What will we be doing? Get "operational descriptions," such as sitting and talking, training the dog, and the like. Find out exactly why these things are being taught, and how it should help you with your specific problem.
- How long will the sessions last? It depends on the problem—severe problems may take longer than relatively simple problems. And, if other needs become obvious once the training has begun, this will extend the time frame.
- Will any special equipment be required? If so, what, and who provides it? Ask exactly what equipment will be used during the training. If shock collars, spike collars, hanging nooses, hobbles, or ultrasonic devices are mentioned, be wary. Get a second opinion from another trainer and don't be swayed by an "I know more than you do" attitude.
- If the problem persists after the program is completed, what happens? Some trainers offer a money-back guarantee if they cannot fix the problem, but most don't. Asking this question will allow you to assess any further classes and concurrent charges if your dog persists in the bad behavior.
- How much will it cost? Always get a fixed rate up front, and preferably in a contract. Make sure that you pay one set rate, and that any additional charges are agreed upon before they are enacted.

Common Problem Behaviors

The following sections detail some of the more common behavior problems and how to deal with them.

Barking

People talk; dogs bark. It's as simple as that—until incessant barking becomes a problem. Excessive barking and barking at inappropriate times can be corrected, but it's much easier to train a puppy than it is to try to correct an adult Basset who has an ingrained habit.

A dog may get into the habit of uncontrolled barking for many reasons. Being confined in a space without any interaction from humans or other animals may cause a lonely or bored dog to bark as a way of drawing attention, even negative attention, to himself. Some dogs are overly sensitive to every sound and movement around them, and they bark when they are startled.

It is no more reasonable to think that you can train your dog to never bark than it is to ask a human to take a permanent vow of

Play is very important for puppies; it helps them learn how to properly interact with other dogs.

Doggy Language

Even though your dog can't speak with words, he can say volumes with his body language. Learning to understand what dogs are saying with their bodies is important, not only to get to know your own dog better, but to predict what strange dogs will do.

- **Confidence:** A confident dog will have an erect stance, standing and walking tall but relaxed, tail up and wagging, and will give you a direct look (usually their eyes will have more constricted pupils).

- **Fear:** A dog who is afraid or concerned will carry himself with a lowered stance and his tail down, sometimes even tucked in, depending on the level of fear or concern about the situation. The tail may wag, but it will likely be a quick erratic wagging, not the lazy sweep of a happy dog. He will likely not look at you directly and may even turn his head away showing you the white of his eye (often with somewhat dilated pupils). He may curl up, or try to make himself appear as small and insignificant as possible. You should never reach out to a dog who is showing fear.

- **Anger, Aggression, or Arousal:** An angry dog will usually raise his "hackles" (the area over the shoulders). This doesn't always mean the dog will be aggressive, but means that he has gone into a stage of "red alert" and is prepared to go to battle at the slightest hint of danger. If a dog has stiff legs and body, tail stuck straight out from his body, a lowered head with ears "pinned" against his head, eyes narrowed and fixed intently, lips drawn into a snarl with raised hackles, he has gone from red alert into war mode. Be wary, do not attempt to touch this dog, and be careful not to make any sudden movements.

- **Playfulness:** The classic tail and butt in the air while the front legs are lowered, also called a "play bow," is a dog's invitation to play. Many dogs will "grin" and their eyes will look open and relaxed. Puppies will sometimes paw the air like a kitten when they are trying to induce their littermates into puppy games. Among dogs, these actions seem to be some sort of indicator that anything that follows should not be taken as a serious attack upon the other dog(s). The bark that some dogs do in play will usually be higher pitched than that of a dog's fear or warning bark.

When dogs (or humans) misunderstand dog body language, trouble is likely to occur. The breeds of dog who look most like their feral ancestors (German Shepherd Dogs, for instance) will be able to show much clearer body language. Those, like the Basset, who are more removed from this wolfish appearance will be more likely to be misunderstood. Their long ears are harder to perk and to flatten, their droopy eyes are harder to read, and their low stature and lumbering gait makes it harder for them to take on the swagger of a lankier dog.

silence. It is fine for a dog to bark to sound an alarm, or say hello, but it is simply not permissible for him to continue to bark after he has made the situation known to his humans.

Do not punish him for barking. Rather, praise him for not barking. Teach him the command "No bark" and praise him when he is silent. Whenever your dog is lying around quietly, say, "No bark," then immediately, "Good dog." After he has barked an alarm, tell him, "No bark." When he has stopped, give him the command "sit" or "down" and, when he complies, praise him. This tells him what you expect of him after he's barked a warning.

Biting (Puppy)

A puppy who is mouthing or biting you or other family members is simply doing so because he has not yet learned the rules of proper etiquette when playing with humans. He may appear to be acting aggressively, but this does not mean he is going to grow up into an aggressive dog. However, it does show that he may have aggressive tendencies, and you will have to learn how to deal with them and focus them in a positive direction. This is where knowledge of dog body language will come in handy. It may be that your puppy is not biting aggressively, but is instead just mouthing you, trying to tell you that his teeth hurt. During the teething age of 4 to 6 months, a puppy becomes a "chewing machine," and he should be provided with lots of chew toys to make this time more comfortable for him.

It is very important that you not react with a physical punishment when your puppy mouths you or bites you in play (or in aggression). If you administer any kind of physical punishment when he bites too hard, he will likely respond in kind. You will be teaching him that he should defend himself whenever someone raises a hand to him, and he is likely to grow up into an aggressive dog.

Instead of physical punishment, as soon you feel his teeth on your flesh (or clothing) yell "ouch" loudly. This will startle him, and he will release your hand. As soon as he releases you, pet him, tell him he is a good dog, and play a game with him in which your hand is not near his mouth. Each time the mouthing occurs, have the same reaction until he realizes that human skin is tender and he can never bite down hard—even during play, and especially not in anger. Make sure that all family members follow the same rules

Set Rules Early

If you don't want your adult Basset to get on the furniture, don't hold him there when he's a puppy. The same goes for sleeping arrangements. If he won't be allowed in your bed later, don't take him there when he's a baby.

when playing with the dog. Don't allow the kids to roughhouse with the puppy, because he will be confused about why it is fine to bite one human and not another.

Coprophagia (Eating Feces)

This is the unappetizing habit of eating stool. Why do dogs do this? Most cases of coprophagia appear to be purely behavioral, but numerous medical problems can cause or contribute to coprophagia. These problems must be ruled out first, before a purely behavioral diagnosis can be made.

- A dog may eat his feces if he's not getting enough food or if the nutrition from his food isn't adequate. Check with your veterinarian to see how much food you should be feeding your dog. Bring the label from his food and review it with your vet to see if he is getting all the nutrition he needs. Your vet may be able to suggest supplements that will satisfy his cravings.

Keeping your Basset active and engaged can help prevent problem behaviors from occurring.

- If a dog is scolded or punished severely for having an accident in the house, he may learn to eat his feces to remove the evidence of his indiscretion. In this case, housetraining him properly and positively will sometimes alleviate the problem.

- A dog who is confined in a small area for long periods of time may eat his feces in order to keep his sleeping area clean. This is an easy fix, because it only takes giving him a larger area when he is alone, exercising him more frequently, and supervising him so that he doesn't have an opportunity to soil his bed in the first place.

- Keeping a kennel area or dog yard full of feces may cause a fastidious dog to eat his own feces as a way of general housekeeping. Sometimes, the smell of so much feces can be enticing as well, which prompts him to eat it. Keeping your yard clean and picking up feces as soon as they are deposited will alleviate the problem.

If all else fails, several additives are available to sprinkle on your dog's food; these will make feces unappetizing to him and will discourage him from eating his stool. Once he has lost the habit, you can stop putting the additive on his food.

Digging

There are many reasons that some dogs dig. It is inherent in some dogs, especially those bred to go to ground while hunting prey. In the wild, dogs have to dig a den or warming chamber to survive cold winters. In the summer, they create a cooling pit by digging beneath the sun-warmed surface dirt. Bassets don't dig any more than any other breed, but they certainly can do a good job of it if they're motivated by boredom or an enticing smell on the other side of the fence!

Dogs who are confined to small areas outdoors usually will dig more than a dog who has a lot of room to explore. Some dogs dig to escape their enclosure. Others dig seemingly for the pure enjoyment of seeing dirt fly. They will move from one area to another, excavating until your yard looks like the surface of the moon. Some dogs dig to hide their bones and toys.

If your dog digs because he is bored, you simply must eliminate his motivation to dig by giving him other ways to occupy his time. Giving him a place where he is allowed to dig can be helpful. Create a sandbox or other area with soft dirt and bury some interesting items in the soil. At first, bury them near the surface so that he can find them easily. Over time, bury them deeper so that he will have to work harder to find them (although, of course, not so deep that he cannot find them, or so deep that he can't get the

scent of them to know they are there). Take him to this area and say, "Dig," then praise him when he finds one of the buried treats. Do this several times, and he'll soon get the idea that this is a treasure trove. When he's inside, bury more treats, and when you let him outside again, say, "Dig," so that he will know that something good awaits him. Soon, he'll lose interest in digging in places where no treats are ever awaiting him, and he'll limit his digging to this approved spot.

If you see him digging in an unapproved spot, tell him sternly, "No dig" and immediately take him to his area and give him the Dig command. Praise him when he does. You will have to continue to keep treats in this area to keep him interested, but in time you can allow more time between placements.

Dog-to-Dog Aggression

Some dogs are more prone to fighting than other dogs. Dogs show aggression for a variety of reasons, ranging from a dog who is genetically prone to aggression, to a dog who was not properly socialized with other animals as a puppy. Some dogs feel a need to defend their territory (their yard, their crate, their home, or even their human). Hormones also can play a large part in dog aggression. Two unneutered males will be more likely to have a spat than would two altered males. A dog who is kept restrained (in a tie-out) becomes aggressive to combat his feelings of helplessness. Many times, a dog who has always been low in the pecking order in a multiple-dog household or environment will develop aggressive tendencies.

The most important thing for you to remember when dealing with a dog who displays aggressive behavior is to never (even unintentionally) give him any positive reinforcement for this behavior. If your dog growls at another, don't stroke him and say soothingly, "It's OK, don't do that." He will understand from the tone of your voice and the touch of your hand that you are praising him for his behavior. Don't pick him up, because that will make him feel helpless, and he will try harder to be a "tough guy" the next time around.

Telling him "Good dog" when he shows aggressive behavior will not help make your dog a good watchdog. All it will do is help to create a mean dog who will be an insurance liability and may end up causing problems in your neighborhood that can be costly as well as heartbreaking.

If your dog shows aggressive behavior toward another dog, it is time to socialize him correctly with other dogs. If you see a dog approaching you, laugh, sing, or talk happily, so that your dog does not sense any apprehension on your part. If you tighten up the lead to pull him closer to you, or start telling him "no" before he has shown any aggression, he will see your action as fear of the other dog. He has no way of knowing that your apprehension comes from not knowing his own intentions. Each time your dog meets another dog and does not display aggression, praise him and pat him. Do not bring treats into the equation when two dogs are together, especially if one might display territorial aggression. Training your dog to sit, go down, and stay when he is around other dogs will help enforce your role as a leader and help him realize his role in dog society.

Fear of Loud Noises

The terror some dogs feel when they hear a loud noise usually can be traced back to an event from their puppyhood, when a traumatic experience occurred at the same time as a loud noise. Sometimes, it is a fear that is picked up from their humans, especially from an owner who is afraid of thunderstorms or other loud events. Fear transference is fairly common from owner to dog, so it is important that you never let your dog sense your fear of anything that you do not wish him to fear as well.

Although you should try to avoid altogether any predictable loud noises (fireworks on the Fourth of July, etc.), you also should attempt to desensitize your dog by exposing him to low-volume noises while you are creating a pleasurable atmosphere for him, either by giving him a treat, brushing him, playing with him, or doing anything that he enjoys. This can be a tape of a thunderstorm, rock and roll music, or a movie with a soundtrack that includes a lot of loud noises (explosions, gunfire, etc.) played on low volume. Gradually increase the volume while you continue with your happy time. If you don't show any reaction to the sounds, and good things are happening to

Discourage jumping up at an early age, to help prevent problems later.

him when he is hearing them, soon the fear will no longer manifest itself at all.

If your dog doesn't respond well to the desensitization, it may be necessary to ask your veterinarian for a tranquilizer to give to your dog when you think loud noises might occur that would traumatize him. Since you cannot always anticipate when a surprise thunderstorm will pop up, or a car will backfire, or a child will toss a firecracker in the street, be prepared to work with your dog to help him through his fears. When the noise occurs, act happy and unconcerned. If your dog sees that you are not frightened, it can help him realize his fears are unfounded. Always be sure your dog has a safe place—his own crate, under your bed, or in a closet—to run to when he is afraid.

Jumping Up

Puppies jump up on us as a way of greeting and expressing their joy at seeing us, and we don't mind because they are little and cute.

However, the same action from an adult dog (especially a large Basset) that tears and dirties our clothes becomes a problem. And because of the Basset's delicate skeletal structure, jumping up also should be curtailed to avoid possible injury. The best way to avoid these types of problems in an adult is to nip them in the bud while they are puppies.

You always must be consistent, so that you don't confuse your Basset. Don't scold him for jumping one day, then pat your chest urging him to "give you a hug" or jump up into your arms the next. Make the decision of what you expect from him, and make sure he knows what that is.

When your Basset jumps up on you, other people, or furniture say, "Off" loudly. You want to startle him, so that he pays attention immediately. Then tell him to sit, and when he does, praise him and give him a treat. He should quickly learn that when he approaches you or others, he should sit quietly and wait for attention from you.

Self-Mutilation

While cats lick themselves frequently to stay clean, dogs rarely do this. If your dog licks himself obsessively, to the point that his fur falls out and his skin is irritated, and he has been checked for parasites or foreign objects caught in his hair or an allergic reaction to food or medication, he is exhibiting stress behavior. This could be a result of his relationship with you or other family members, with other animals in the household, lack of exercise, boredom, or because he is unsure of his station in life. Mouthing himself, chewing himself, and excessive licking are the only methods he can employ to relieve tension (much as a nervous human will chew his fingernails or wring his hands).

It is very important to build your dog's confidence. Teach him simple commands and praise him effusively when he does them correctly. Praise him for everything he does well, and avoid scolding him. Spend more time playing with him, and take him for walks. Getting more exercise may help if the problem manifests itself from stress caused by boredom or loneliness.

Keep in mind that any behavior that makes you uncomfortable should not be ignored. Seek professional help immediately for the sake of you, your family, and your Basset.

ADVANCED TRAINING
and ACTIVITIES
With Your Basset Hound

ot every dog is suitable for every activity. Basset Hounds, because of their nature and physical makeup, won't excel at the same types of sports as a Border Collie or a Labrador Retriever will, but they can compete in many fun activities. Hunting, showing, tracking, search and rescue, therapy, and even agility are all possibilities, as long as you're willing to put in the dedication, training, and money it takes to compete with your Basset.

YOUR DOG: YOUR PARTNER, YOUR FRIEND

Before we discuss all the different activities you can enjoy with your Basset buddy, an important reminder: Remember why you purchased a dog in the first place—for companionship. Throughout this book, you will see your dog being referred to as a "pet," regardless of what other activities he enjoys on the side. He should always be your pet before he is anything else. Don't let points, ribbons, titles, or awards become so important to you that you forget that this slobbering, happy-go-lucky fur-foot is a living, breathing creature, dependent on you not only for food and shelter, but also—more importantly—for love and companionship. He should always be your pet first and a show or performance dog second.

ORGANIZED ACTIVITIES FOR YOUR BASSET

Agility

As the name implies, agility is a sport best suited for the more agile Basset. While most Bassets give the impression of being better in the lumber and drool categories than agile and athletic, your Basset may surprise you with his abilities.

Agility is the most rapidly growing dog sport in England, Western Europe, and the United States since its debut at Crufts Dog Show in 1979. Spectators and exhibitors alike thrill to the excitement of watching a dog's and handler's enthusiasm as they race against the clock.

Loosely modeled on the type of track laid for equestrian stadium jumper competitions, a canine agility course is run by a dog (off leash) and his handler. In the United States, several national organizations sanction agility competitions. The international rules and regulations call for the highest level of skill, speed, and physical ability from the canine competitors. Domestic (US) varieties of the sport call for less actual agility (lower jump heights, smaller obstacles) and focus more on the handling aspects.

The obstacles common to both skill levels include:

- A-Frame
- Dog Walk
- See-Saw
- Collapsed Tunnel
- Pause Table
- Tire or Hoop Jump
- Various Types of Jumps

The obstacles used on an agility course were designed both for safety and aesthetic appeal for spectators. In regards to the safety factors, jumps have easily displaceable bars to avoid injury to the dogs who touch them. All obstacles have "contact zones" painted, so the dog can be trained to stay in safe areas, and they are roughened for good traction in any kind of weather (no matter the weather, the show must go on!). For aesthetics, the jumps and obstacles are brightly painted and have a sort of "circus" atmosphere.

In competition, the obstacles always are arranged in random configurations, so that they always are unique from trial to trial.

Agility Tidbit

The first Basset to claim an AKC agility title was Ch. Juley von Skauton. To see photos of Bassets enjoying their agility run (along with other great Basset agility links), check out www.agilitybassets.com.

The handler directs her dog around the course in a sequence that is predetermined by the judge. Dogs competing on lower levels of entry have fewer complications, but it is still considered good training if the handler can prove her dog can competently follow the course in a reasonable amount of time. As the dog (and handler) becomes more adept, he can enter higher levels of competition, in which the courses increase in complexity, and coordination between handler and dog becomes imperative. A specific time is set by the judge, and the course must be run within that Standard Course Time (SCT).

The rules are simple for agility. Handlers can offer an unlimited number of commands, encouragements, or signals, but are not allowed to touch either the equipment or the dogs. Dogs are "faulted" for taking down jump bars, failing to put their feet in the contact zone on contact equipment, taking obstacles out of required sequence, or stopping before an obstacle. Time penalties are assessed for dogs not finishing within the SCT.

Competition is made equal by allowing dogs to only compete against dogs of similar height. The number of height divisions and

Some Bassets may surprise you with their ability to handle obedience jumps like this one.

the ranges of dog heights vary from organization to organization. Be sure that you are very familiar with each group's rules and registrations before entering their competitions.

Canine Good Citizen (CGC)

The Canine Good Citizenship Certificate is awarded under rules established by the American Kennel Club. It is open to all breeds of dogs, including mixed breeds. It is a two-part program designed to teach responsible dog ownership to owners and to certify those dogs who have the training and demeanor to be reliable, well-behaved members of their families and communities.

The CGC test is not a competition, and dogs are not given a number score, but instead graded on a "Pass" to "Needs More Training" scale. The purpose of the CGC Program is not to provide an avenue of competition, but simply to ensure that your dog can be a respected member of the community, because he is trained to act mannerly in the home, in public places, and in the presence of other dogs. Dogs who pass all 10 items of the test receive a certificate from the American Kennel Club, a tangible proof that the dog is indeed a "good citizen." (This certificate will be of importance should you decide to use your dog as a therapy dog at hospitals, nursing homes, and retirement facilities.)

The CGC test has ten parts:

- *Test 1: Accepting a Friendly Stranger.* An examiner approaches you and your dog and talks to you in a friendly manner, possibly shaking hands or making some sort of body contact. Your dog cannot show any aggression or defensive posturing.
- *Test 2: Sitting Politely for Petting.* The dog allows the examiner to pet him while he talks to you in a friendly manner. Again, the dog cannot show aggression, overexuberance or enthusiasm, or defensive posturing.
- *Test 3: Appearance and Grooming.* The dog must allow a stranger to groom and examine him.
- *Test 4: Out for a Walk.* This demonstrates the dog's ability to be easily controlled while walking on a loose lead. It doesn't matter which side you choose to walk your dog, although traditionally, he should be on your left.
- *Test 5: Walking through a Crowd.* This test demonstrates the dog's ability to move about politely in pedestrian traffic and that he is easily kept under control in public places while on

Obedience Classes

No matter what activities you want to eventually enjoy with your dog, obedience classes are a good place to begin. Certainly, a dog who has been through at least basic obedience is easier to live with and may, in fact, be happier because it gives him a chance to know exactly what he needs to do to please you as he learns what your basic commands really mean. If you decide you won't be trying for obedience titles, you can be a little less structured with your training and focus more on the bonding aspect of the classes.

lead. These people will be doing all the things people might do in a public place—opening umbrellas, walking on crutches, swinging a cane, crossing suddenly in front of you and your dog. Your dog should not pull at the leash, jump at the people, or show excitement, fear, or aggression.

- *Test 6: Sit and Down on Command/Staying in Place.* This test demonstrates that the dog has had basic obedience training and will respond to the handler's commands to sit and go down, and he will remain in the place commanded by the handler. These commands are not only convenient but sometimes necessities in unusual situations, as well as in normal life routines. The examiner will ask you to have your dog sit and then lie down on command. You will be asked to

With patience and training, there are plenty of fun activities you can participate in with your Basset.

Obedience Tidbit

To date there is only one OTCH Basset, OTCH Buzz Taylor's Goober, although many Bassets have claimed other Obedience titles.

A Basset is a scent hound who will follow his nose without hesitation if he picks up an interesting smell.

tell the dog to stay, then you will step away from the dog (about 25 feet [7.6 m] or so) and call the dog. The dog should stay until called, and come when called. Unlike formal obedience competition, repeating a command is allowed.

- *Test 7: Coming when Called.* This test demonstrates that the dog will come when called by the handler—another extremely necessary command that can save your dog's life.
- *Test 8: Reaction to Another Dog.* This test demonstrates the dog can behave politely around other dogs. Most dogs will come in contact with other dogs and animals at some point in their lives, sometimes on a routine basis, especially if they are show or performance dogs.
- *Test 9: Reaction to Distractions.* This test demonstrates the dog is confident at all times when faced with common distracting situations.
- *Test 10: Supervised Separation.* This test demonstrates the dog's ability to maintain its training and good manners when left with a trusted person or stranger. Your dog must remain calm if you leave it briefly. The examiner will direct you to secure the dog to some object and then go out of the dog's sight. The dog may move around and show interest in his surroundings,

but he must not whine, bark, pull, or otherwise show distress. An important point to note is that the dog is not left alone but is left under the indirect supervision of a stranger. You can interact with the examiner before you leave, so that the dog is aware that he is not being abandoned and that you trust this stranger.

Recovering his poise after excitement is also part of the test. You will be asked to play with your dog and get him to play with you. You should then be able to immediately calm him down.

Obedience

No one who has shared his life with a Basset will ever associate the word "obedient" with this breed. While some breeds were selectively bred for their willingness to be obedient and please their owners no matter what, generations upon generations of Bassets were bred to simply stick to a scent without distraction. This gene is the same one that will cause a Basset to totally ignore his owner's voice if he is intent upon following a good smell or tracking down a sound. Pleasing themselves is always their foremost concern, with pleasing their owners usually coming in a firm second. You should be aware of this when you choose a Basset as your Obedience dog. Although some wonderful working Bassets can give the other breeds a run for their money, seldom will a Basset be in line when class placements are awarded. The people who train Bassets for Obedience do so for the pure joy of working with their dog, and the challenges that working with a less-than-obedient hound will invariably bring.

The Winning Attitude

A true show dog is born, not created. From his first toddling steps in the whelping box, a winning show dog has a "look at me" attitude lacking in his littermates. Without this spark, this "something special," even the best dog will often be beaten by a lesser dog who carries himself like a showman.

In obedience trials, a dog is judged by his or her ability to obey specific commands. The varying levels in obedience classes range from the novice Companion Dog (CD) through open, Companion Dog Excellent (CDX) to utility, Utility Dog (UD).

For each level of class, a dog must earn (or qualify for) three "legs" to achieve a title. Each leg will have the dog competing for at least 170 out of 200 possible points.

- In the Companion Dog class, each dog is judged on heeling on and off lead at varying speeds, sitting, staying with other dogs on command while the owner steps away from him, and also standing for a brief examination by the judge.
- The Companion Dog Excellent class requires the dog to work completely off leash, perform all the exercises mentioned

above for extended lengths of time as well as jumping obstacles and retrieving.

- The Utility Dog must complete the above requirements but obey visual commands instead of verbal ones. He will have more difficult obstacles and maneuvers to negotiate, as well as perform a scent test.

Don't forget that you and your dog should be using obedience competition as a fun and bonding experience. Remember to have fun, and make sure that your dog is enjoying himself as well. It's easy to get wrapped up in trying to achieve perfect scores and forget that you're both there to enjoy your comradeship. Your partnership should be obvious to everyone who sees you. Your dog should obey you because he loves and respects you and wants to please you, and not because he fears you or fears your displeasure if he fails.

A show dog must allow you to place his feet and his head while he is being "stacked" for examination.

Becoming a Champion

To become a US champion, a dog must win 15 points awarded by judges at AKC-sanctioned dog shows. Computing points is complicated, because points differ not only from breed to breed, but from one section of the country to another. The more dogs of your breed and sex that you compete and win against, the more points you win, along with that coveted purple ribbon. No dog can win more than five points at one show. Wins of three, four, or five points are called "majors" and among your 15 points must be wins at two "major" entries. The rest of the points can be made up of either more majors (if you're really lucky, and you have a superior dog and catch a lot of breaks) or single points won at smaller entry shows.

Each of the Best of Breed winners in each breed will compete with other winners in their Group for a chance at the Best in Show title. There are seven AKC Groups: Sporting, Hound, Working, Terrier, Toy, Non-Sporting, and Herding.

To become a champion in Great Britain, the dogs who win each class compete for Challenge Certificates (CCs), males and females separately. Once you have three CCs from three separate judges, your dog moves up to champion. As in the US, after the CCs have been awarded, the Best of Breed winners from each group are judged to find Best of Group. Then these winners go on to be judged for Best in Show. Although most of the same breeds are recognized in Great Britain as are in the United States, the groups have different names. They include: Working, Utility, Terrier, Gundog, Hound, Toy, Pastoral, Rare Breeds, and Imported Register.

Field Trials

Don't forget that Bassets are born hunters. Field trials are competitions that highlight the Basset doing what he was bred to do: hunt small game, especially rabbits. Those who consider themselves "field trial addicts" say they enjoy their sport not only for the exercise and the pleasure of socializing with other Basset aficionados, but for the pure joy of watching a dog do what he was bred to do. They all agree that the thrill of seeing their dog follow a trail the way his ancestors have done for generations is a true sight to behold.

Remember that, to be a true champion in the field, your dog must not only have the desire to hunt (something inherent in most Bassets), but he must be able to be controlled while in the field. He also must be in outstanding physical condition, because some hunting terrain is very hard and dense, and an out-of-condition

dog can suffer great physical damage.

Very few areas offer training for field trials, but most Basset owners and trainers in other fields (pardon the pun) can likely direct you to Basset owners in your area who field-trial their dogs. They will probably be more than happy to invite you and your dog to work and hunt with them.

Showing (Conformation)

One of the most important aspects of being a good breeder is competing in conformation exhibitions with the best examples you have produced from your breeding program. Every dog is judged according to the breed standard (explained in detail in the Appendix). Judges determine the best dogs of the day according to their movement, their appearance when standing, and their overall condition. Although maybe not always the "showiest" breed at a dog show, any well-bred, well-trained, and well-groomed Basset Hound who loves the show ring can always be a contender for Group and Best in Show placements.

A puppy cannot be shown in either the United States or Great Britain for points until he is 6 months old, but you should be able to find some puppy matches nearby for good experience while he is waiting for that 6-month birthday. Matches are run in the same style as a "real" show but in a much more relaxed and informal setting. Entry fees are usually just a few dollars instead of the large fees now charged for point-show entries.

Only unspayed bitches and intact males can compete at AKC conformation shows. This harkens back to the original purpose of dog shows, which was to select those dogs that would produce the best offspring. Many exhibitors think this rule is outdated and should be abolished or at least changed to allow sterilization in some circumstances, but rules are rules and they must be abided by until they are changed. However, the only reason to keep your dog intact is for showing purposes, unless you are planning to engage in a well-planned breeding program.

No matter how excited you are about showing your puppy, be careful not to burn him out on showing by dragging him hither and yon while he is too young to really be competitive against the "big boys." Most dogs don't truly come into their own until after they're 2 years old. With body maturity also comes the mental maturity necessary for a show dog to compete day after day, week after week. Many a lovely puppy with the promise of turning into an equally lovely adult has been ruined by being pushed too hard and too fast into a show career.

Although dog shows should be fun days, remember to watch your dog closely at all times. Bad experiences, such as being jumped on by smaller yippy dogs or larger snarly ones, can wreck a show dog's career before it starts. Make sure your own dog is a good sport as well and knows how to be a good citizen.

What It Takes to Win

Before you start, you need to become familiar with the Basset Hound breed standard and make sure that your particular dog has no faults that could prevent him from competing. Then, he must learn basic manners as well as some basic obedience before you can expect him to consistently win. He must:

With training and conditioning, a Basset can become a champiom in competition.

- Learn to walk quietly at your side inside and out of a ring.
- Be willing to allow you to place his feet and his head while he is being "stacked" for examination, and hold whatever position in which you place him until you tell him it is okay to move.
- Stand quietly on the ground and on a table while a judge examines him thoroughly (including his teeth and private parts).
- Learn to tolerate his peers without showing any aggression or even play tendencies.
- Learn to trot at whatever speed you ask him, matching his speed to yours, on a loose lead or with pressure on the leash.
- Learn what "no sniff" means—keeping his nose off the ground

Tracking may just be the ideal activity for your Basset.

Sports and Safety

Although you and your dog will both be healthier, happier individuals if you spend time together doing some sort of performance activity, remember to keep safety issues first and foremost in your plans. Hunting, obedience, agility, and other canine sports all can put wear and tear on your Basset's body. Before you and your dog undertake any strenuous new activity, check with your vet (as well as your own doctor) to be sure that no one's health will be compromised by the increased activity. Start out slowly, and don't over-exercise. Follow all the rules and regulations of any organized event or training classes you attend, and avoid any circumstances that could lead to danger. Never push your dog to complete a course or trial if he appears ill or limping. Serious, even permanent damage can easily be done. A canine athlete is as likely to have a sports injury as any human athlete. Make sure that you are prepared to take care of him in any emergency, and be aware of the potential problems and safety issues in any sport in which you choose to train and work.

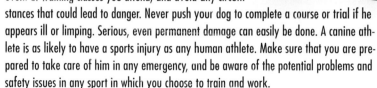

in the ring (ignoring the tantalizing aromas of dropped bait, "seasonal" girls, and hormonal boys).

- Learn to keep all four feet on the ground even though your pocket reeks of some of his favorite treats.

A conformation dog isn't just bred and trained, he must be conditioned as well. The most well-bred Basset, trained and handled to perfection, won't stand a chance against an equal competitor who has been excellently conditioned. For some dogs, conditioning may require a strict exercise and diet regimen. For others, brisk walks with their owner may do the trick. Whatever method you use, be careful not to overdo it. Muscles are good in the right amount and place, but your Basset shouldn't look like the canine version of a champion bodybuilder. He should be in a proper muscle tone and weight for his breed and sex. His skin and hair should be in good condition as well. This takes a while to achieve, but can be maintained easily with the proper diet and bathing regimen.

Professional Handlers

If you want to handle your dog in the ring yourself, it's a good

What Not to Wear

We all have seen the shows on TV aimed to outfit normal people for everyday lives. But what about the dog person? What outfits and clothing are considered proper for all the different events you can share with your dog?

No matter what the event (unless perhaps the Best in Show ring at Westminster), it is always best to dress conservatively. No dangly or jingly jewelry, no glitter, nothing to detract from your dog (including having loose change in your pocket). You should always wear comfortable shoes with a nonskid sole. Make certain that the sole is not soft rubber that can grip the ring mats too well and cause a tumble. You should choose an outfit with pockets for bait and show paraphernalia, or you can purchase a clip- or pin-on bait pouch and choose clothing that has a good attachment point.

- **Conformation:** Remember that you are a background for your dog. You're not the one who should catch the judge's eye, but you should create a vignette with your dog that will bring her eyes to you both. If you are showing only one dog, you should choose a color of outfit that will coordinate well with him but not hide him. Jewel tones work really well with almost all colors of dog. Black or white make excellent backgrounds for the opposite color of dog. Prints, florals, and polka dots should be chosen carefully, because they can detract attention from your dog. Be careful of choosing a color that is too close to the color of your dog (unless he has a horrible topline that you'd like to camouflage), because this can make him appear to fade away. In the show ring, as any other place, the adage "out of sight, out of mind" holds true. Most people wear outfits that would double as appropriate clothing for a job interview.

- **Hunting and Tracking:** Certainly, anyone who goes into a field that is filled with hunters with guns should wear at least one (if not several) bright orange or other fluorescent-colored piece of outerwear. Footwear should be chosen depending on the type of terrain and what type of walking you may be required to do. If you are competing or training for a tracking test at a rural location, you should likely wear at least one item of clothing in an easily visible color. Clothing should be loose, layered, and comfortable. No matter the weather, take along at least a light jacket in case of sudden rain showers.

- **Obedience and Agility:** Clothing should be neat, well tailored, and allow for full range of motion for the arms and legs. Footwear depends on whether the trial is at an outdoor or indoor location.

idea to take your dog to some handling classes. Not only will your dog benefit from the socialization experience, but also the handling skills you'll learn will give you an edge in the ring. You'll learn not only ring protocol, but show terminology, dress codes, and how to present your dog to his best advantage.

If you decide you don't want to show him yourself, professional handlers are available in almost every area of the country. You can either turn your dog over to them until he is finished, or take him from show to show and hand him off ringside (most handlers prefer to have the dog in their possession for at least a week or so before a show, for grooming and training preparation). If you decide to hire a handler, be certain you choose someone who is well known for his love and attention for the dogs in his care. Many handlers become so popular that they have large "strings" of dogs who go with them to each show, making it less likely that your dog will get any one-on-one attention during the time he's being shown, except for grooming and training. Make certain the handler you choose believes in letting dogs be dogs, and allows them adequate exercise and fun time.

Therapy and Service Dogs

Once your Basset has received his Canine Good Citizenship certification, he will be welcomed into almost any hospital, nursing home, school, and child and adult care facility. There he can visit the sick, elderly, and rehabilitation patients and provide canine education programs to children. But a dog doesn't have to have a certificate to be welcome at most places. He does, however, have to prove himself capable of handling these types of situations, and he cannot do that without some background work on your part. Not only is it necessary that he has the right temperament to be trustworthy around the elderly, young, and infirm, but he must have learned some basic manners. He also should have been exposed to a great number of unique situations that will prepare him for the unusual things that he may encounter on his rounds as a therapy dog. If you can't find a training class for therapy dogs in your area, you can do much of the training yourself. Basic obedience (with emphasis on sit, stay, and down) and field trips with your dog to public places will help turn him into a dog who will bring smiles to the faces and hearts of many people.

Some of the places you might consider taking your therapy-dog-in-training include:

- Shopping centers or malls, where he can encounter shopping carts, escalators, elevators, people carrying umbrellas and canes, and possibly even people in wheelchairs.
- A busy section of town, to let your Basset get used to strange noises and the hustle and bustle of a lot of strangers.
- Hospitals and nursing homes, to visit adult ambulatory patients who understand they are part of the dog's training. This will allow the dog to come in contact with people in wheelchairs, using walkers and canes, and walking while having IVs attached to them.

Once your dog has learned some basic commands and become accustomed to being among strangers (including some with unusual smells), and among the various equipment commonly

With proper training, Bassets can make excellent therapy dogs.

Playing games with your Basset will strengthen the bond between you—and keep him from getting bored.

found in medical facilities, he will be ready to join you for some of the most heartwarming and rewarding experiences of your lives.

Many people are confused about the difference between therapy dogs and service dogs. Although both provide a great service to the people whose lives they touch, a therapy dog is not a service (or assistance) dog.

Service dogs are specially trained to serve one owner who needs their help to enable them to live independent lives. Service dogs include guide (or leader) dogs for the blind; hearing dogs who alert their owners to sounds; mobility-assistance dogs who may either pull a wheelchair or provide support for a person; seizure alert dogs who alert their owners to oncoming seizures; and other dogs specifically trained to provide various types of support for their owners. A service dog is entitled to go into any place his owner goes, whenever he is needed, no matter what. A therapy dog must provide paperwork and receive validation and an invitation before he is allowed into many public facilities.

Tracking

The ability of a dog to follow a scent that is hours or even days old, over inhospitable terrain, and sometimes in inclement weather

is forever a mystery to humans. Most Basset owners who train their dogs to track believe that this is the ideal activity for any Basset. The dogs get to use the wonderful sensory perceptions with which nature and heredity have blessed them, and no other animals are harmed or killed in the process.

Not just any dog, no matter how well it tracks, can enter a competition for its Tracking Dog (TD) or Tracking Dog Excellent (TDX) titles. First, the dog must be certified as qualified by a person approved by the AKC to judge tracking events. To receive this certification, the dog must pass a certification test of a complexity equivalent to that of the TD test, and the test must take place under the conditions to be expected at an approved AKC test.

It's not the simple matter of taking your dog into a field and asking him to follow a scent. The tracking course is a complex network, carefully laid by skilled track-layers. And what elusive treat will your Basset be tracking? Lost children? Stranded campers in need of rescue? Nothing so dramatic, I'm afraid. For the TD test, a wallet or glove is the usual article of choice.

After a dog has achieved his TD title, he can begin working on a TDX. The TDX course is longer and offers more obstacles, changes of terrain, and crossing of tracks. As an additional distraction, four personal items are dropped along the track.

The AKC also offers competition events in Tracking (Variable Surface Tracking Test, or VST) for dogs who have earned their TD or TDX titles.

FUN AND GAMES

All work and no play will make your Basset a really bored and unhappy fellow. People who regularly play with their dog develop understanding and communication with their dog that is far different from that learned during regular training.

Find-the-Treat

Since Bassets are such good trackers, Find-the-Treat is an excellent game for them. Put them in a down or sit-stay position, and hide tasty treats in the yard (or a room of the house if it's bad weather). Give them the command to "Find It" and watch their tails wag as they hone in on their prizes.

Follow-the-Leader

Grab a tasty treat and take off, urging your dog to follow you as you go over obstacles, such as wading pools, footstools, and other challenges. A great start before training for agility later on.

Hide-and-Go-Seek

Put your dog in a stay position and hid out of sight. Then call your dog to you. The better he gets at it, the better your hiding places must be.

My Dog-Can–Do-That

This is a board game published with training tips (written by Dr. Ian Dunbar and Terry Ryan). It has cards describing tricks or performances of varying levels of difficulty. The more difficult the performance, the more points for correctly performing it. You and your dog will have great fun competing with all your dog friends. The game is sold through a wide variety of dog book and dog supply retailers.

HEALTH

of Your Basset Hound

n general, the Basset Hound Is a healthy breed. Exercise and good diet seem to be the keys to good health for a Basset, because inactivity and obesity, combined with the breed's skeletal and digestive system, can result in a number of health issues. If you choose a dog whose parents were thoroughly screened for genetic health problems, feed him a well-balanced diet, and give him proper exercise, you should look forward to a long, healthy, happy life together.

CHOOSING A VETERINARIAN

Responsible dog owners know that one of the most important people in their dog's life is his veterinarian. Over the years, you will be placing the life of your best friend in her hands. Make certain you choose a vet you can trust—one who will truly listen to you.

You should ask your friends, family, and co-workers for recommendations. People who love their pets will be able to direct you to a vet who truly cares about animals and their welfare, and who doesn't see her clinic only as a business.

When you've narrowed down your choices, make an appointment to talk to each veterinarian (and the office staff) in person. Ask questions, and be wary of any clinic that doesn't have someone willing to take the time to answer your questions and make you feel comfortable. Some questions to consider are:

- What are their regular and emergency hours?
- Do they have tattooing or microchip services?
- Do they have boarding facilities?
- Do they have financing available in case emergency costs are not payable immediately?
- Do they offer any alternative practices? If not, can they direct you to a clinic that could provide those services?

Remember that just because you start with one veterinarian

doesn't mean you should stay there if you are uncomfortable with her or any aspect of your pet's care. If you don't feel that your new vet is truly listening to you, or considering your observations and opinions regarding your pet, it's time to try someone different. Your vet should be willing to listen to your observations about your dog and consider your feelings and opinions when making decisions regarding your pet's care.

Tips for Choosing the Right Vet for Your Dog

- It's a good idea to always check with the Veterinary Medical Board to see if any complaints have been filed about the veterinarian you are considering
- Make sure your new vet likes dogs. You might ask in conversation what kind of dog they have themselves. This can open up the avenue to find out if they truly are a dog person.
- Ask if the veterinarian is familiar with the treatment of Basset Hounds.
- Find out what they have available for after-hours emergency care. If they do not provide emergency service, get them to refer you to a clinic that does, for emergencies.
- Check if somebody will be with your pet through the night in case of an illness or accident that requires an overnight stay.
- Ask if the office accepts insurance plans if you have one, or credit cards or payment plans if you don't.
- Watch the interaction between vet and vet technicians. Are they friendly? Does courtesy and politeness rule the day?
- Trust your nose as well as your instincts when choosing a clinic. Although it's inevitable that sometimes a vet clinic will have animal and medical odors, no overwhelming smells should suggest that animals are not kept clean while in their care.
- And last, but perhaps the most important, rely on your gut instinct. If you feel uncomfortable, keep looking.

PUPPY'S FIRST VET TRIP

You should have your new puppy thoroughly examined by a veterinarian within a certain length of time after purchase. You should have been made aware of any major health problems before the purchase, but your vet may uncover something that was missed. If this happens, don't panic. Some problems your vet might

Did You Know?

Although proximity shouldn't be a factor in routine medical care, it can be the difference between life or death for your pet in the case of an emergency. If the vet you choose as your general practitioner is quite a distance from your home, it would be a good idea to choose a "backup vet" or emergency pet hospital that is closer to your home.

find on the initial checkup are actually quite common—internal parasites (especially roundworms) may show up on the fecal examination the veterinarian will do during your visit. All that's usually required is a single dose of dewormer (most vets use a paste formula that puppies actually find quite tasty) and a return checkup in a few weeks to make sure the worms are all gone and the puppy hasn't picked up new ones. Other internal parasites that plague dogs include whipworms, tapeworms, hookworms, and other pests such as coccidiosis and giardiasis. While its true that most of these are easily treated, it's very important to take care of the situation as quickly as possible, because the added depletion to the systems of small puppies and adults in a stressed condition can cause their health to be severely compromised.

One of the most important people in your dog's life is his veterinarian.

Your vet also might find a small umbilical hernia. Umbilical hernias are quite common, especially in puppies born to first-time mothers who either bite the umbilical cord too close to the stomach or damage the umbilical cord through excessive licking. Most are due to delayed closure of the umbilical ring. These will almost always get smaller and likely will disappear by 6 months. If it doesn't disappear on its own, the surgery to repair it is relatively simple and can be done quite easily when the dog is spayed or neutered.

If you've chosen a male, the vet should make sure that both testicles have descended into the scrotum. If not, neutering will be more costly and more invasive.

Once you're sure your puppy is healthy, you can relax and begin to enjoy each other's company. Your vet will likely set you up with a schedule for checkups and vaccinations as well as other preventative medicine.

YEARLY EXAMS FOR YOUR BASSET

Just as you should see your doctor on a regular basis, so should your dog have regular physical examinations. Although the techniques may differ between canine and human doctors, the

Your Basset puppy should have his first veterinary exam shortly after you acquire him.

The Importance of Spaying or Neutering Your Basset

First, let's look at the big picture: Every day in the United States, approximately 10,000 children are born. Every day in the United States, approximately 70,000 puppies and kittens are born. If you do the math, you can quickly see that there will never be enough homes for those animals. Bringing more into the world doesn't make a lot of sense. Unless you are dedicated to this breed, willing to spend the time and money it takes to devote your life to bettering it for future generations, leave the breeding to professionals and do the right thing: Spay or neuter your pet!

Now, we'll look at the smaller picture. If you love your Basset, and want to do all you can to ensure his good health, spaying and neutering can drastically improve his health and life expectancy. Worried that your pet will become fat or lazy when he is spayed or neutered? Stop worrying—that's a myth. Want to make some extra money selling puppies? Any breeder will laugh at that one! After proper genetic testing, pre- and post-natal care, and the appropriate care of the puppies, you'll more likely find that your bottom line is red instead of black.

Spaying a female eliminates the possibility of uterine and ovarian cancer and greatly reduces the risk of breast cancer. Neutering a male reduces the risk of both prostate enlargement and prostate cancer. Neutering also will make your pet more affectionate and less likely to roam, get in fights, or become lost. You also won't have to worry about keeping your carpet and furniture clean because of your female's bi-annual heat seasons (Basset girls are notorious bleeders), and you won't have to worry about your boys going nuts when the unspayed girl next door goes into season. Spaying or neutering won't alter your pet's basic disposition, but it can make him less likely to have hormonal temperament issues.

When you look carefully at both pictures, I think you'll agree that sterilizing your pet will make you both a lot happier and make your pet a lot healthier. It's a clear choice.

reason is the same—it's better to prevent disease than treat it. Also, the earlier a malady is detected, the better the chances of a successful treatment and a full recovery.

An annual examination will help your Basset's veterinarian assess the health of your pet and recommend care. Although you can become aware of certain problems at home (often while grooming or stroking your dog), some problems are not noticeable except to a trained medical expert. Annual physicals usually include checking temperature, pulse, respiration, weight, eyes, ears, mouth and throat, coat and skin, lymph nodes, abdomen, bones and joints, heart and lungs, and the perineum and reproductive organs. Bring along a fecal sample, so that the vet can check for internal parasites.

Your veterinarian should check your pet's teeth during all well-pet visits, and she can tell you when your pet needs a thorough dental cleaning, which in most cases will require anesthesia. If your pet has bad breath that can't be explained by something he ate, chances are very good that he either has tonsillitis or his teeth need a deep cleaning.

If you're not taking your dog to a professional groomer or trimming his toenails yourself when you groom him, you should ask your vet to trim your dog's nails while you are at the clinic. Most vets will do this for a very nominal fee. Long toenails are not only a hazard to your clothing and skin, but can be easily snagged and torn, which can cause pain and discomfort to your pet (to say nothing of the blood stains on floors and clothing—nothing bleeds more copiously than a torn nail!). Long nails also place undue stress on the joints of the paws and can cause long-term problems.

Vaccinations have saved the lives of millions of dogs.

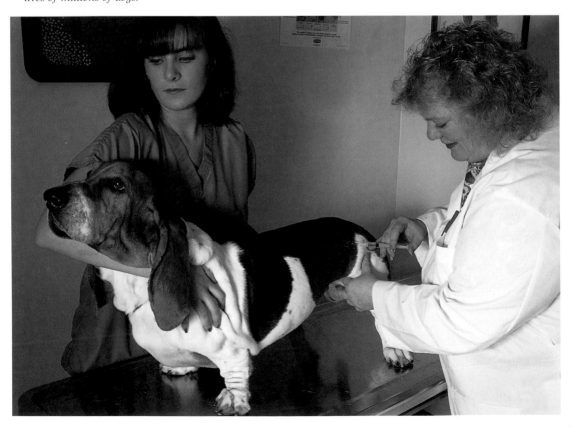

VACCINATIONS

Vaccinations have saved the lives of million of dogs. Once dreaded canine diseases are now nearly extinct because of the efficacy of vaccinations. For many years, it went without question that puppies began a vaccination routine at 6 weeks, receiving booster vaccinations for the next 6 weeks, then receiving vaccinations on an annual basis throughout their lifetime. Today, many vets are questioning this vaccination regime. Not all dogs react well to vaccinations—skin reactions or serious systemic reactions are possible—so you should discuss a vaccination schedule with your veterinarian after doing as much research as possible on the subject. Together, you can decide what is the best schedule for your particular dog.

Diseases to Vaccinate Against

Your veterinarian may provide routine vaccinations for canine distemper, infectious canine hepatitis or adenovirus, leptospirosis, parvovirus, coronavirus, Parainfluenza, Bordetella, Lyme disease, and rabies.

- Distemper is a highly contagious, often fatal virus that affects a dog's respiratory, gastrointestinal, and nervous systems. Generally, this virus spreads as an airborne infection, so vaccination is the only effective control.
- Adenovirus (also known as infectious hepatitis) is a viral disease that affects the liver and cells lining the blood vessels, causing high fever, thirst, loss of appetite, abdominal pain, liver damage, and hemorrhage.
- Leptospirosis is an extremely contagious disease (often carried by rats and mice) that spreads through contact with the nasal secretions, urine, or saliva of infected animals, and can affect humans as well. The ailment causes inflamed kidneys, fever, vomiting, and diarrhea. Liver damage also can occur in severe cases.
- Parvovirus is an unfortunately very common and deadly viral infection whose symptoms include diarrhea, fever, and vomiting. Parvovirus usually is seen in younger dogs, and can kill puppies very quickly.
- Coronavirus is a highly contagious viral infection of the gastrointestinal tract whose symptoms are almost identical to those of parvovirus.

At Risk for Bloat?

Researchers say that deep-chested dogs who weigh over 50 pounds seem more prone to bloating, and an adult Basset certainly fits this description. The cause of bloat is unknown, but implicated dietary factors include food particle size, frequency of feeding, speed of eating, aerophagia (swallowing too much air), and an elevated food bowl. Talk to your vet about recommendations for avoiding this terrible condition in your Basset. Never delay when bloat is suspected—it can be fatal within the hour!

- Parainfluenza virus is one of a number of infectious agents that cause what is often called "kennel cough." The disease is highly contagious and attacks the respiratory system, resulting in a dry, hacking cough.
- Rabies is an always-fatal infection of the central nervous system that affects all mammals, especially raccoons, bats, skunks, foxes, domestic dogs and cats, and humans. Since rabies poses a serious public health threat, it is imperative that your puppy be vaccinated. Most states require it.

Remember, most vaccines must be given over a period of time and require multiple veterinary visits, including annual boosters. Check with your veterinarian and follow her suggestions for a vaccination schedule.

PROBLEMS SPECIFIC TO THE BASSET HOUND

Although other breeds can develop these problems, and Bassets can suffer from problems that are uncommonly seen in the breed, these are the most probable health issues in the Basset Hound.

Allergies and Skin Conditions

Some Bassets may be prone to allergies, dermatitis, and seborrhea. More has probably been written about the various skin conditions that plague the canine world than any other aspect of dog ownership. The skin is an excellent barometer for the overall health of a dog. Dry, itchy, red skin with scaly hairless patches and flakes of dandruff can be indicative of many things, from basic dry skin that can be treated by adding a teaspoon of vegetable oil to your pet's food each day, to demodectic or sarcoptic mange that must be treated by your veterinarian.

Poor skin quality also can be a sign of allergic reactions to almost anything your pet comes in contact with. Experts agree that over 50 percent of dog allergies are a reaction to something in their food. Before you spend a lot of money on allergy testing and inoculations, try switching your pet's food to something with a different base ingredient. If your dog food has a chicken base, try feeding one that is made from lamb and rice or beef. With pet supermarket shelves full of good-quality food, you should be able to find something that will suit your Basset's needs.

Bloat (Gastric Torsion)

Bloat is a condition in which a dog's stomach twists and traps gas inside. Unlike human anatomy, a dog's stomach is suspended in his body like a hammock. In a human, a build-up of gas can pass up or down, but a dog has more difficulty passing air or gas that is trapped in the stomach. The pain caused by bloat is excruciating,

The Basset Hound is one of the breeds at risk for bloat; make sure you know the signs of this dreaded condition.

An itchy Basset may have anything from dry skin to allergies to external parasites such as fleas.

and treatment must be timely—even then it may not be possible to save the dog.

How will you know if your dog is in danger? A dog who is experiencing gastric torsion will appear uncomfortable, restless, and he'll get a "worried" expression. Symptoms will progress to aimless pacing and rapid, shallow panting. He will swallow, salivate, and he may try to vomit but it will be futile if the stomach has already torsioned. If you see his stomach visibly increasing in size, he is already in serious trouble. His gums may become pale, he may have a rapid heartbeat, and he will go into shock if not treated immediately.

The exact cause of bloat is still unknown, but the most important thing to remember is that bloat is an emergency situation. If your dog shows any symptoms of bloat, seek emergency veterinary care immediately. If your dog survives bloating, he will have to be on a special diet for the rest of his life, because he always will be more susceptible to bloating.

Every Basset owner should have on hand an over-the-counter rapid gas reducer containing simethicone, which breaks up gas bubbles. Ask your vet what she suggests, and administer it according to her directions. You also can take emergency measures that can make the difference between life and death. Stand the dog upright and burp him just as you would a baby. If you don't have someone to help you hold him up, place his front feet up on a sofa, chair, your chest; whatever is most comfortable for him. Begin to pat him, starting low on either side of the belly and working your way up the rib cage. If he belches in your face, be grateful, and keep burping him. If his legs start to tremble, you may have to let him down for a minute to relieve the pressure on his back legs but continue to burp until he seems comfortable and no more gas is passing. Remember, if you have someone to drive, you can do this while in the car on the way to the vet. If you suspect bloating, there's no time to delay—minutes can mean the difference between life and death for your dog.

If he does not pass gas soon, it is because the tablet isn't working, you are not burping properly, or the stomach has already twisted. Make sure you have called ahead to your vet—this is an emergency situation, and they should be prepared to take him straight to surgery. There's no time to leave you in the waiting room while they prepare. If you think your dog is more at risk, discuss it with your vet before it reaches an emergency situation.

An annual examination will help your Basset's veterinarian assess the health of your pet and recommend care.

To avoid herniated disks, it's very important that you not let your Basset jump up or down from heights.

Blood Diseases

Two blood diseases can affect the Basset: Von Willebrand's Disease (vWD) and canine thrombopathia (CTP). These diseases are potentially life threatening, so early diagnosis and treatment is vital.

Von Willebrand's Disease (vWD)

vWD is found in humans, dogs, and other mammals. Caused by a deficiency or abnormality of the blood proteins that control platelet activity, a dog with this disease has a tendency to hemorrhage. Researchers believe there may be a relationship between vWD and hypothyroidism, another problem commonly found in Bassets. There is no way to determine whether vWD is hereditary or acquired. The test can only determine positive, negative, and a percentage of affliction. It is suspected that thyroid medication, as well as the functioning state of the pet's thyroid

When to Consult Your Veterinarian

You should consult a veterinarian immediately if you notice:

- Abnormal behavior, such as sudden lethargy in a usually active pet, hyperactivity in a normally sedentary dog, or aggressive or vicious episodes in a pet who is usually docile and friendly.

- Loss of appetite.

- Excessive weight loss or gain (it's a good idea to weigh your pet every week or so — this also helps keep your dog's diet in check before a problem with obesity begins).

- Abnormal discharge from your dog's eyes, ears, nose, or other body openings.

- Abnormal swelling or lumps anywhere on the dog's body; female dogs should have monthly breast exams just as human females should. Spayed females are not as likely to develop mammary tumors, but they still can occur.

- Excessive thirst and/or urination.

- Limping or "favoring" a leg.

- Difficulty getting up or lying down.

- Excessive scratching or shaking of the head, or abnormal scratching, biting, or licking any part of the body.

- Loss of hair, bald spots, large amounts of dandruff, scaly patches, or a dull, lifeless coat.

- Excessive tartar deposits at the gum line or on the teeth.

- Bad breath (which can be a sign of tonsillitis), or infected teeth or gums.

- Open sores, especially those that don't heal even after treatment.

- Abdominal swelling or pain, especially if the dog has eaten something out of the ordinary including animal fats, table scraps, or cooked bones.

- Difficulty breathing.

- Vomiting or diarrhea, especially if blood is found (you should remember that blood isn't always red; sometimes it will appear dark brown or black and tarry if it is present in the stool).

Not only does your dog need to see his veterinarian on a regular basis, at least for a thorough annual checkup, but you should establish a routine for checking him on a regular basis throughout the year as well.

gland may have an effect on vWD test interpretation, resulting in false negative or false positive results. You may want to discuss this with your veterinarian. Dogs who have been diagnosed with vWD will forever have the disease and its effects. It can be controlled through various treatments and medications, in much the same way as it is controlled in humans.

Canine Thrombopathia

CTP is a platelet dysfunction that may keep a Basset's blood from clotting properly. It is harder to test for than vWD, since definitive testing requires not only specialized equipment but medical personnel trained to use it. Thus, testing is limited to only a very few laboratories at this time. Treatment is the same as vWD.

Symptoms of a Blood Disorder

What should you look for if you suspect your Basset is affected with a blood disorder?
- Bleeding from the gums or other mucosal surfaces, including nosebleeds
- Blood in urine or feces, including recurrent bloody diarrhea

A Basset's long, floppy ears are particularly prone to ear infections.

Check your Basset for fleas and ticks after he's been outside.

- Prolonged heat seasons in female Bassets
- Lameness mimicking panosteitis
- Hematomas—pockets of blood beneath the skin, often seen in ears that have been scratched because of ear mites or other irritants (although hematomas can appear on any part of the body)
- Prolonged bleeding from minor injuries, like cutting nails, loss of puppy teeth, cutting the umbilical cord, dew claw removal, during or following whelping, tail injury, and the like
- Red spots on a pup's tummy, which may be subcutaneous hemorrhages, known as petechia
- Severe bleeding during or following surgery

If your dog shows any signs of abnormal bleeding, contact your veterinarian immediately. Early diagnosis is the only key to possible survival.

Cancer

Cancer isn't one specific disease. It's a generalized term for more than 200 different types of malignancies that can affect almost any part of your Basset's body. Cancer in dogs is much like cancer in humans, and dogs can be treated the same way as are humans, using much the same methods and treatments. At one time cancer was a death knell for dogs, but new treatments are being put into action every day that can buy you extra time with your buddy, and possibly heal him so that he is able to lead a long and normal life.

According to the Veterinary Cancer Society, here are common signs of cancer in small animals (you'll notice that the signs are quite similar to cancer in human beings):

- Abnormal swellings that persist or continue to grow
- Bleeding or discharge from any body opening
- Hesitation to exercise or loss of stamina
- Sores that don't heal
- Weight loss

Tips for a Healthy Basset

- Acquire your Basset from a reputable source, one from which you are certain the parents received adequate prenatal care and genetic testing.

- Don't overfeed your Basset. Obesity is harmful to your Basset Hound's heart, spine, and joints, and makes him more susceptible to other health issues.

- Keep a good grooming routine. Religiously clean your Basset's ears once a week, trim toenails once every 2 weeks, and check for full, impacted anal glands. And don't forget his teeth!

- Give your Basset regular heartworm medication (as directed by your vet) and check for fleas and ticks.

- Immunize your Basset for distemper, parvovirus, hepatitis, leptospirosis, and parainfluenza.

- To avoid spinal injury, do not let puppies climb long flights of stairs or jump off objects such as beds, couches, or porches, especially before 1 year of age.

- Never let your Basset wander loose in the neighborhood.

- A Basset is safest in a secure, fenced area, or on a leash. Never allow your dog outdoors unsupervised and unprotected.

- Loss of appetite
- Offensive odor
- Difficulty eating or swallowing
- Persistent lameness or stiffness
- Difficulty breathing, urinating, or defecating

If you notice any of these symptoms, have it checked out by your veterinarian. Just like humans, early detection is the key to a complete and speedy recovery.

Ear Infections

Because a Basset's long, heavy ears lay close to his head, they do not allow sufficient circulation of air. Ear infections often develop if owners are not diligent about cleaning their Basset's ears every week. See Chapter 5 for more information on how to clean your Basset's ears.

Eyelid and Eyelash Problems

Bassets are prone to ectropion (a turning out of the eyelids), which results in a dry cornea, and entropion (a turning in of the eyelids), which causes lashes to dig into the surface of the eye. Luckily, both conditions can be corrected surgically.

Glaucoma

This eye disorder often is found in the Basset Hound breed. Symptoms include painful, bulging eyes and sensitivity to light. All Bassets should be checked by a licensed ophthalmologist on an annual basis after 2 years of age. If their eyes test clear, they can be given a registration number by the Canine Eye Registration Foundation (CERF). Any Basset used in a breeding program should have a current CERF number. If you are purchasing a puppy, be sure to ask if both parents are CERF certified.

Early detection and treatment is the key to this disease. Glaucoma that has been present for less than 48 hours can be effectively treated (this is considered an emergency treatment). Although only a small percentage of dogs regain vision in an eye that has glaucoma, treatment helps relieve the extreme pain associated with this condition. If you wait longer than 48 hours, treatment may no longer be effective. Treatment in the form of oral medication and/or eye drops often is needed to control glaucoma for the rest of your pet's life. If the eye is permanently blind, your

You might want to explore some alternative therapies for your Basset.

vet may suggest surgery to relieve increased eye pressure instead of long-term medication.

Hypothyroidism

A sluggish thyroid gland (hypothyroidism) is the commonest endocrine gland disease of dogs; male and female dogs are affected equally. The thyroid gland consists of two lobes located at the base of the neck. This gland produces thyroxine, a hormone that regulates the body's metabolic rate, which is the rate at which it burns calories. Most cases of hypothyroidism stem from the dog's own immune system attacking thyroid gland tissue. This condition is called autoimmune thyroiditis.

It is common for dogs with hypothyroidism to gain weight while eating moderately. Also, adequate levels of thyroid hormone are necessary for hair to grow. When hormone levels are low, hair will grow sparsely over the lumbar region as well as the back of the rear legs and the tail. The dog's coat is often flaky and dull, the undercoat will be sparse, and even hair color may change. Hypothyroid dogs also commonly have excess black pigment in the skin of their groin. Sometimes this pigment is present over much of the body, and the skin becomes oily and thickened. Broken toenails and toenail infections are common. An important clue to suspecting thyroid deficiency is that your dog won't scratch as he would if the skin and hair changes were from fleas, allergic skin, or other skin disease.

Although the following symptoms also are seen with other disorders, they may be present in a dog with hypothyroidism:

- Mental dullness or depression
- Cold intolerance
- Slow heart rate
- Constipation
- Anemia
- Muscle weakness and atrophy
- Nerve disturbances
- Edema
- Stunted growth
- Slowed clotting of the blood
- Joint pain and swelling
- Ear and skin infections

Treatment can bring about a total reversal of the symptoms, although it may take several tries to find the right level of medication that your dog will have to take daily for the rest of his life. Hypothyroidism is a genetic health problem, so it isn't wise to

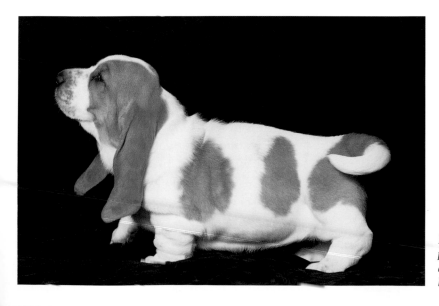

Bassets are particularly prone to obesity, which can cause a variety of other health problems.

169

Holistic Helpers

You can keep the following natural remedies in your first aid kit:

- Cayenne pepper: apply to wounds to help stop bleeding
- Calendula gel: a topical treatment for wound healing
- Arnica gel: a topical treatment for sprains, strains, bruises
- Comfrey ointment: a topical ointment for wound healing

breed hypothyroid dogs or their normal littermates. When the disease is diagnosed early and given proper treatment, you can expect your Basset to live a totally normal life.

Intervertebral Disk Disease

Herniated disks are common in Bassets, especially if they frequently jump from high places onto their front limbs. Intervertebral disk disease occurs when the jelly-like inner layer of a spinal disk protrudes, or herniates, into the vertebral canal and presses on the spinal cord. Compression of the spinal cord may be minimal, causing only mild back or neck pain that a stoic dog won't let you know about, to a severe injury, which causes paralysis, loss of sensation, and lack of bladder and bowel control. The worse the injury, the more likely it will be irreversible. Bassets were bred to have short, thick legs—basically the result of an abnormal development of cartilage. The intervertebral disks in Bassets gradually become more like cartilage than fibrous tissue, thus increasing the risk of disk rupture.

Symptoms can range from a visible, mild discomfort when you touch his spine or he attempts to walk or lie down, to paralysis in extreme cases. The type of treatment your vet prescribes will vary depending upon the severity of the injury. In some mild cases, anti-inflammatories will be administered to help take down swelling and eliminate pain. In more severe cases, surgery may be advised. It's very important to seek medical help at the first sign of injury, because the longer you wait, the more damage may be done to your dog's spinal column.

It's very important that you not let your Basset jump up or

down from heights, be careful how you carry him when he's a puppy, and try to avoid letting him go up and down stairs on a regular basis.

Obesity

Obesity is especially harmful for long-backed breeds like Bassets. Their long spines and knuckled joints cannot handle the stress of excess weight. See Chapter 4 for more information on how to prevent and handle obesity in your Basset.

Panosteitis (Pano, Wandering Lameness, Puppy Limp)

Pano is an inflammation of the long bones of the leg, often seen in Bassets from 5 months to 2 years of age. Because dogs outgrow pano, it is not considered a serious health problem; however, x-rays should be taken to ensure that the problem is indeed pano and not a different problem that might require medical attention. Lameness caused by pano may move from one leg to another and can last from a week to 6 months or more. Bassets with pano should not be exercised until symptoms disappear.

INTERNAL AND EXTERNAL PARASITES

Vigilant parasite control, both external and internal, is important for both the comfort and health of your dog. He should have a fecal exam done every time he visits the veterinarian, and appropriate parasite control measures should be taken, especially if your dog has to be treated routinely for flea or worm infestations. Your veterinarian can tell you the biggest potential problems where you live, what treatments work best in your specific area, and what preventative measures you should take for the specific parasites your pet seems to pick up most frequently.

Internal Parasites

It is very true that all dogs will at some time during their life have worms, no matter how vigilant their owner is about parasite control, so don't panic if your dog gets a positive fecal exam.

Many types of internal parasites and worms exist. They include:
- Giardia (Giardia lamblia): Probably the most common of the canine parasites—it's estimated that half the puppies in the

Did You Know?

Aloe vera can provide temporary relief for hot spots, bites, and many other skin irritations. Besides being non-toxic, aloe vera is also bitter so it may discourage licking, which can slow healing.

Step-by-Step Instructions for the Heimlich Maneuver

- *Check for signs of choking:* Hard coughing, eyes bulging in panic because he can't breathe, and pawing at the mouth.

- *Clear the mouth.* If your Basset is conscious, pry open his mouth and look inside. Hold one hand over the top of the mouth, using your thumb and forefinger to press against the lips to get the mouth open. Pull the bottom jaw down with your other hand. Use your thumb and first finger to sweep the mouth and remove any foreign objects.

- *Place your dog on his side.* If you can't see anything in his mouth, turn him on his side, with his head lower than his rear. Put something like a pillow under his rear end.

- Find the bottom of the rib cage, where the ribs meet in the middle (sternum). Then go a few fingers width below, toward the belly.

- *Press in and up.* If your dog is small, put one hand at the spot you found, and the other behind the dog's back for support. If your dog is large, use both hands to press sharply in and up. Keep doing it until he expels what he was choking on. Try the next step if this one doesn't work.

- *Do artificial respiration, if necessary.* If he's unconscious, keep him on his side, head lower than his rear. Extend the head gently up and out. Pull the tongue to the side. Do the compressions from the last step, twice. Then check the mouth for the object. Close the mouth, extend the head up, and give two breaths through the dog's nose until you see the chest rise. Repeat the compressions, the mouth check, and the two breaths until the dog is breathing again.

No matter what happens next, get to the vet immediately. If possible, have someone else drive so that you can be on your way to the vet while you are still working with your dog.

United States are affected.

- Roundworm (Toxocara canis): The most common worm. Nearly all puppies are born with roundworms, which they acquire from their mother. Older dogs are less likely to be affected, but they can pick them up from infested soil (the main reason you should always pick up your pet's feces immediately).

- Hookworm (Ancylostoma caninum): Can be passed to humans. Dogs with hookworm infestation will usually have blood in their stool, will likely lose weight, and will show gastric distress.

- Whipworm (Trichuris vulpis): The hardest of all the worms to destroy, both in your dog's system and in infested soil. Severe infestations can give a dog colitis and can prove fatal.

- Tapeworm (Dipylidium caninum): Tapeworms are visible in your dog's stool. You may see what looks like tiny grains of rice around your dog's anus. These are actually dried tapeworm segments. If you dog has fleas, he likely has tapeworms. Regular dewormers will not work against tapeworms.

- Heartworm (Dirofilaria immitis): Your dog should stay on a good heartworm preventative throughout his lifetime. As the name suggests, these worms travel through your dog's bloodstream to his heart, where they attach to the lining, doing great damage to the heart muscle as well as blocking arteries. The preventative is easy; the treatment can be severe and costly. An added benefit of keeping your dog on heartworm preventative is that it will also help prevent other types of internal parasites as well.

See your veterinarian for treatment and prevention options for these internal parasites.

External Parasites

Your Basset will likely pick up fleas and ticks on his forays into the great outdoors. While fleas are simply pesky to most dogs (except for those with sensitive skin or severe allergies), ticks can create a serious health hazard for you and your pet if you live in an area where Lyme disease is found.

Alternative therapies can be combined with modern medicine to treat your pet.

Your veterinarian can tell you if Lyme disease is a problem in your area, and he can vaccinate your dog against the disease if necessary.

Flea and tick control can be applied topically or given orally on a once-a-month schedule that is usually sufficient for most pets. However, keeping your pet flea free in some areas, especially those with a hot, humid climate, may require a

Your Basset will depend on you in any emergency, so remember to stay calm.

bit more work by treating the surroundings. Several wonderful species-specific insect growth regulators are on the market; these do no harm to the environment and work upon contact to make insects sterile. Although you may have to spray with a chemical insecticide occasionally, remember that these harsh sprays are not species-specific, and you could end up creating an even greater problem if you kill "good" bugs along with the "bad." If you do use chemicals for flea prevention, be sure to keep them away from your pet, and don't let him in the yard until the spray has completely dried or into the house until it is aired out (you might do well to follow those same instructions yourself!).

COMPLEMENTARY AND ALTERNATIVE VETERINARY MEDICINE (CAVM)

This field covers a growing number of healing methods that pet owners are finding useful in not only keeping their pet healthy, but treating injury and illness. Complementary and alternative medicine is a group of diverse medical and health care systems, practices, and products that are not presently considered a part of conventional medicine. If alternative therapies interest you, you should look for a veterinarian who will put both modern medicine and ancient tried-and-true methods to work to make your pet's life longer and healthier. These ancient methods include (but are not limited to) the following.

Acupuncture

Acupuncture is the Chinese practice of inserting needles into specific points (acupoints) along the "meridians" of the body. Acupuncture is used to relieve pain, to induce surgical anesthesia, and for preventative as well as therapeutic purposes. The insertion of the needles stimulates the acupuncture points and alters the flow of chi (the vital force or energy of the body) throughout the body.

Aromatherapy

Aromatherapy uses the essential oils of plants to promote relaxation and help relieve the symptoms of specific ailments. Essential oils are extremely concentrated and very fragrant extracts that are steamed from the blossoms, leaves, or roots of various plants. These oils can be applied through massage, as compresses on the skin, diffused into the air and inhaled, or mixed with water as a bath. Essential oils are so concentrated that they should be considered extremely toxic if they are ingested.

Ayurvedic Medicine

Ayurvedic is a form of medical care practiced mainly in India. In this belief system, health is considered to be a delicate balance between the body's physical, emotional, and spiritual systems; illness is proof of an imbalance. Illness can be detected by reading the pulse and the tongue. Treatments can include nutrition, massage, natural medications, meditation, and other natural approaches.

Chiropractic

Chiropractic is a system of healing based on the idea that the body has an innate self-healing ability. Subluxations of the joints are believed to interfere with the body's ability to maintain good

health. Through manipulations of the spine and other joints and muscles, the body is brought back into balance, so that the neuromusculoskeletal system can again function smoothly.

Energy Medicine

Energy medicine includes therapy using an energy field (which can be electrical, magnetic, sonic, microwave, infrared, or acoustic) to detect and treat illness. A practitioner can identify imbalances in the energy fields of the patient's body and, using a chosen energy, can attempt to correct them.

Environmental Medicine

Environmental medicine is an approach to health that focuses on the role of allergens (both dietary and environmental) on a patient's well-being. Proponents believe chronic illnesses can be controlled or improved with the judicious use of environmental medicine.

Herbal Medicine

Herbal medicine involves the use of natural plants, or substances derived from plants, to treat illness, prevent disease, and enhance the body's function. All parts of the plant may be used in herbal medicine, including the bark, leaves, stems, and roots. These constituents can be prepared in many ways to make tonics, pills, powders, and extracts. No governing body oversees the strengths of these herbal remedies (or how they are gathered, prepared, or prescribed). Therefore, to avoid over- or underdosages, they should be used only under the guidance of a practitioner who is familiar with herbal medicine.

Holistic Medicine

As the name implies, this is a philosophy that views the patient as a "whole" body, instead of just a particular disease or a list of symptoms. It takes into consideration that a patient's mental, emotional, and spiritual state can affect his overall condition—and that nutrition, environment, and lifestyle can positively or adversely affect a patient's body and can contribute to an illness. Holistic practitioners usually treat patients with a blend of traditional forms of treatment, such as medication and surgery, with additional alternative forms of treatment such as acupuncture, chiropractic, or herbal medicine.

Homeopathy

A philosophy of "like heals like." In this branch of medicine, treatments are composed of substances that, in their undiluted state, can produce the symptoms of the disease in an otherwise healthy patient. The substances are diluted greatly in solutions that are then given to the patient. Homeopaths also usually believe that a patient's mental, physical, and emotional state must be addressed along with his body's medical symptoms, and these aspects must be treated along with the symptoms for a full recovery to take place.

Kinesiology

Kinesiology is an investigation of the muscle-gland-organ link in order to find the cause of illnesses. Practitioners of applied kinesiology believe muscles reflect the flow of a body's energy or chi and that one can determine the health of body organs by measuring muscle resistance. Once the problem has been identified in this manner, a number of different treatment techniques may be employed to strengthen the involved muscles and restore good health to the patient.

Many common household plants can be toxic to your dog. Make sure none of the plants in or around your home can pose a danger to your Basset.

Massage

Massage is a systematic therapeutic stroking or kneading of the body or part of the body. The manipulation of a body's soft tissue structure can reduce tension and stress, increase circulation, aid the healing of muscle and soft-tissue injury, control pain, and promote an overall sense of well-being.

Nambrudripad's Allergy Elimination Technique (NAET)

Nambrudripad's Allergy Elimination Technique (NAET) is an approach to detecting and eliminating allergies. It combines kinesiology and oriental medicine to clear the symptoms of allergic reactions. The technique involves the stimulation of those specific acupuncture points along the spinal column that are associated with individual organs of the body.

Giving Your Basset a Pill

If the medication can be given with food, wrap it in a piece of cheese and let him swallow it. If not, open his mouth and place the pill as far down his throat as possible, then close his mouth gently with your hands.

Reflexology

Reflexology is a type of therapy that works on the theory that different regions of the feet correspond to particular body systems. Treatment involves the manipulation of specific areas of the feet to eliminate the energy blockage that produces disease in the associated organs.

Shiatsu

Shiatsu is a Japanese technique that uses finger and thumb pressure on precise body points to encourage a proper flow of chi (energy) throughout a patient's body.

Tellington Touch (T Touch)

T Touch is a method of training named after its developer, Linda Tellington-Jones. This technique uses a combination of specific touches, lifts, and movement exercises that can enable an animal to learn new behavior more easily, promote optimal health, and correct inappropriate behavior by eliminating many fear and negative reactive responses.

Therapeutic Touch

Therapeutic touch is a method of healing in which, despite its name, no actual physical contact is involved. The practitioner aligns and balances the patient's natural energy field by moving his hands just above the patient's body. The healer attempts to focus positive energy to the patient to balance and unblock positive energy flows.

SAFETY AND FIRST AID

In case of an accident or emergency, you should be familiar with your pet's baseline readings to evaluate how severe an emergency is and to have that information ready to give to your emergency veterinarian when she is contacted. These baseline readings should include:

- *Your pet's rectal temperature:* Normal body temperature for a dog is between 99°F (37.2°C) and 102.5°F (39°C). Learn how to take your dog's temperature before you're in an emergency situation, so that you will be comfortable doing so. Using a well-lubricated thermometer, properly shaken down to below 96°F (35.5°C), gently insert the bulb end of the thermometer into your Basset's rectum. Hold it firmly but gently in place for about 1 minute. It's a great help if someone will hold your dog's head to keep him standing in place.
- *Color of skin and gums:* Some dogs routinely have paler or brighter gums than others, but they should never be bright rosy red or pale gray. Pale gums can indicate anemia or shock. Dark red ones can mean poisoning or a high fever. A yellow tinge is an indicator of liver dysfunction.
- *Heart rate:* The normal heart rate for a Basset is between 60 to 140 beats per minute. Check your dog occasionally when he is healthy to get a more accurate count. Place your fingers on the femoral artery that runs along the thigh bone on the inside of the rear leg, about halfway between the hip and the knee. Using a stop watch or clock with a third hand, count heartbeats for 10 seconds, then multiply by 6.
- *Respiration rate:* Most dogs breathe 10 to 30 times per minute.
- *Capillary refill time (CRT):* The amount of time it takes for tissue to resume normal color after pressure has been applied and removed. To test CRT, firmly press your thumb on the gum near a canine tooth. Remove your thumb and note how long it takes for the white mark to return to pink. If it takes longer than 2 seconds, the situation may be critical. This is an indicator of circulatory (heart) problems, shock, or dehydration.
- *Dehydration test:* Pinch skin and pull up from shoulders and

release; dehydrated skin holds the shape of the pinch; normal skin will resume its normal shape

- *Responsiveness:* Normal dogs are alert, curious, and responsive. If he has a slow response to touch or sight, seems sleepy or disoriented, is having seizures, or has no response to even pain stimulation (pinching between toes is a good stimulation when checking for response time), get him to your veterinary clinic immediately.

What's in Your First-Aid Kit?

It's a great idea to keep a first-aid kit around the house for emergencies. You can use an old shoe box, a plastic container, or anything else that fits your needs. Make sure that you write "First Aid" on the side and keep it within easy reach.

Every well-stocked first-aid kit should have the following:

Average Age Equivalents

Dog Age		Human Age
8 months	=	13 years
1 year	=	16 years
2 years	=	24 years
3 years	=	28 years
5 years	=	36 years
7 years	=	44 years
9 years	=	52 years
11 years	=	60 years
13 years	=	68 years
15 years	=	76 years

- Note card with phone numbers for your regular veterinarian, emergency veterinarian, and local and national poison-control center.
- Note card with baseline health information for your pet including weight, temperature, blood panel results, and current vaccination records.
- Humane muzzle, or old panty hose for making a makeshift muzzle (even the most well-behaved dog will bite when he is in pain).
- Material for bandaging injuries, including:
    - ~ Sterile gauze pads, various sizes
    - ~ Stretchable and nonstretchable gauze (differing widths)
    - ~ Elastic bandage
    - ~ Plastic wrap for sealing wounds against dirt and air
    - ~ Bubble wrap (for splinting)
    - ~ Sterile tape
- Blunt scissors (for trimming fur from wounds and cutting bandages/tape)
- 3% Hydrogen peroxide (for cleansing wounds and to induce vomiting)
- Tweezers or hemostats for removing foreign objects
- Lubricants (petroleum jelly, mineral oil)
- Styptic powder
- Thermometer
- Antiseptic liquid soap
- Hot water bottle, heating pad, or hot/cold packs
- Cotton balls
- Sterile saline contact lens solution (for flushing wounds)
- Karo syrup or honey (for treating shock victims)
- Buffered aspirin (for pain)
- Antihistamine (for itching, stings, or bites, and as a sedative if needed)
- Antidiarrheal medication

Poisonous House and Garden Plants

These common household plants are poisonous to dogs to some degree. Before you purchase new plants for your yard, always ask a garden expert if a plant is poisonous when ingested. While some plants are less toxic than others, and may not be potentially life-threatening, it's best to avoid all toxic plants when possible. The

Dangerous Plants

The list below shows what part of each plant is the most toxic.

- Amaryllis (bulb)
- Apple (seeds, can be fatal—cyanide poisoning occurs when eaten in large quantities)
- Apricot (pits)
- Autumn crocus (bulb)
- Azalea (all parts)
- Bleeding Heart (foliage, roots)
- Buttercups (all parts)
- Caladium (leaves, roots, possibly fatal if large amounts ingested)
- Calla Lily (all parts, can be fatal)
- Castor Bean (seeds)
- Cherry Tree (leaves, twigs, seeds, tree bark, can be fatal due to cyanide poisoning if ingested)
- Chinaberry (all parts, can cause fatal convulsions)
- Crocus (all parts)
- Crown of Thorns (all parts)
- Daffodil (bulb can be fatal)
- Delphinium (seeds and young plants)
- Dumb Cane (all parts)
- Elderberry (all parts, especially roots)
- Elephant's Ear (all parts)
- Four-o' clock (roots, seeds)
- Foxglove (leaves, seeds, can be fatal)
- Golden Chain (seeds, can be fatal)
- Holly (berries)
- Hyacinth (bulb, can be fatal)
- Hydrangea (all parts)

- Iris (underground stem, leaves)
- Ivy, Boston (all parts)
- Jonquil (bulb)
- Lantana (all parts, can be fatal)
- Larkspur (seeds, young plants, can be fatal)
- Lily-of-the-Valley (leaves, flowers)
- Mistletoe (berries, can be fatal)
- Morning Glory (seeds)
- Mother-in-law's Tongue (leaves)
- Narcissus (bulb)
- Oleander (leaves, branches)
- Peach (pits, can be fatal due to cyanide poisoning)
- Peony (roots)
- Philodendron (all parts)
- Poinsettia (leaves, sap, stem, can be fatal)
- Rhubarb (leaves and blades; leaf stalk is harmless)
- Skunk Cabbage (all parts)
- Tobacco (leaves)
- Wisteria (seeds, pods)
- Yew (seeds, foliage, bark, can be fatal)

most common symptoms seen in pets who have ingested a toxic plant include swelling or irritation of the tongue, nausea, paralysis, salivation, and staggering. The list below shows what part of each plant is the most toxic.

If you believe that your dog has ingested a toxic plant, get him to a veterinarian immediately. Wrap him in a blanket to avoid chilling from shock, and keep the dog as quiet as possible en route. Try to keep the head lower than the body to allow poisons to drain from the mouth. Take a portion of the suspected plant with you for positive identification. Do not administer first aid if the dog is convulsing or unconscious.

If your veterinarian is unavailable, call the national Animal Poison Control Center for advice on what to do for your pet. It is the only one of its kind in North America, and it acts as a 24-hour-a-day hotline center for animal poisoning inquiries from the United States, Mexico, and Canada. Have your credit card handy when you dial, because a nominal fee is charged to cover their expenses. The toll free number is 1-800-548-2423.

If your pet shows only a mild reaction, and you wish to administer first aid, you should induce vomiting using an emetic. If your dog does not vomit, you should attempt to dilute the poison

A well-stocked first-aid kit could save your dog's life in an emergency situation.

in his system by giving him milk, egg whites, vegetable oil, or Milk of Bismuth. Activated charcoal, crushed into milk or egg whites, is a good remedy for mild poisoning.

Lost Dog!

Almost every dog owner will at some point experience the trauma of realizing their dog isn't where he is supposed to be. What should you do if you can't find your dog? First of all, don't panic. Keep your wits about you and think like a dog. The chances of finding him are quite good if you act quickly and efficiently.

- *First, search your property thoroughly.* Dogs can get into some mighty strange places, and sometimes they will sit patiently waiting to be rescued instead of making noises to alert you to their situation.

- *Walk the neighborhood, talk to everybody, and leave your phone number.* Go to each house in the area where your Basset was lost and talk to the residents. If possible, quickly make up a flyer with a small photo of your pet, a description, and your contact information, preferably a cell phone that you can have with you at all times. (For safety's sake, it's not a good idea to post your home address on flyers, but be sure a contact phone number is available.) Leave one of these brochures with each person you see, and if someone isn't home, leave it attached to their door.

- *Make a lot of noise while you walk around the neighborhood!* Animals can hear you from great distances. Have all your family members call your Basset's name, and if your pet has a favorite squeaky toy bring it along and use it to help you make familiar noises. Carry a box of your pet's favorite biscuits, chews, or other treats and rattle it loudly while calling his name. As important as it is to make lots of noise, it's equally important to remember to stop and be quiet occasionally, in case your dog is making sounds to try to get your attention.

Giving Your Basset Liquid Medication

Using a needleless syringe, squirt the medication into the back of the dog's mouth. Tuck the syringe neatly down the "cheek pocket" of the dog's mouth and hold the jaws closed with the lips firmly together. Don't cram it down his throat, and keep his head tilted upward. After giving the medication, stroke his throat gently.

- *Bring a powerful flashlight (even during daylight hours) for checking in dark spaces.* An injured dog will likely hide in a dark place and may not come out to you if he is scared or possibly so injured he cannot move or make a sound. Check underneath cars and houses, inside storage sheds, garages, in dumpsters, and behind outbuildings and woodpiles.
- *Place strong-scented articles outside your home to attract your pet.* Animals find their way by scent as well as sound (especially true when it comes to Basset Hounds!). Place some of your dirty clothes such as sweaty gym socks, t-shirts, or jogging suits on the ground. Check back often to see if your dog may be waiting patiently beside them. If the weather cooperates, crate other family pets outside in a safe and secure area so that your lost pet can possibly smell them and return. They also may make noise that would attract their lost comrade.
- *Call local veterinary offices* to see if your pet was injured and taken to any of these offices or clinics for treatment.
- Contact and visit your local animal control, humane societies, and animal shelters, including those in surrounding areas. Leave flyers with a description of your pet and contact information. Check back with them daily, because they usually operate on a volunteer basis, and different people may be manning the office each day.
- *Post as many flyers as possible about your lost pet* within a 1-mile radius of where he was lost. Put ads in local newspapers, and ask your local radio station if they could mention your situation on the air.

You should be very aware that dangerous people in our society prey upon victims by using "found" pets as a ploy. Often, they will have stolen the pet in the first place to have a reason to contact you.

Your aging Basset will still need exercise—check with your vet to see how much is healthy for your dog.

For that reason, you should never respond to a "found-pet" contact alone. Take a friend with you and meet in a public place. And never arrange to meet the person at your home, unless it is a neighbor whom you know well.

When you have found your pet, remember to go back and take up all the flyers you have posted, perhaps replacing a few with a new flyer expressing words of thanks to those who cared enough to send good thoughts, if not actually help with the recovery.

An Ounce of Prevention

Just as with veterinary medicine, prevention is the best option for keeping your Basset from getting lost in the first place and for increasing your chances for a successful recovery in case he is somehow lost:

- Always keep your Basset confined to a fenced area when he is outdoors, unless he is on a leash or supervised in some other manner. Check fence perimeters and gates often to find potential escape routes.
- Always transport your Basset in a pet carrier to avoid the chance of him escaping in case of an accident, or if a car door is left open and unguarded a second too long.

- Have good, clear photos of your dog scanned and on your computer ready to use as quick identification.
- Have him microchipped or tattooed, so that a rescuer will have a way of contacting you.
- Train your dog to come to one specific sound, no matter what. A whistle, a specific phrase, or a dog whistle. Perhaps use that phrase or sound before every meal so that the dog associates it always with something positive and is more likely to come to it when he finds himself outdoors and on his own.
- Always keep your dog's rabies tag on his collar, not only as a means of identification, but as proof that he has been inoculated, in case he is accused of biting someone. In areas that are in a Rabies Alert stage, if your pet is picked up without a current tag, he could be euthanized and sent for testing before anyone realizes he is a beloved pet.

If you ever lose your dog, act quickly, but remain calm—and try to think like your dog would to determine where he is most likely to go.

• Spay or neuter your dog to alleviate the wanderlust that many animals feel when their hormones start raging.

By taking the proper precautions from the beginning, and having a good plan of action in case the worst-case scenario occurs, your dog will have an excellent chance of spending all his nights where he belongs—at home in the arms of his family.

Holidays With Your Hound—How to Keep Him Safe

The holidays bring about an entirely new set of worries when it comes to keeping your pet healthy. Things that seem safe and enjoyable can actually be quite toxic and potentially deadly to your Basset.

Parties can be a threat to your pet unless everyone who attends is dog savvy and knows the rules about what is acceptable for dogs to eat and drink. Some people think it's funny to give a dog an alcoholic beverage. They wouldn't think a drunken dog was so funny if they had to sit up with him all night, or pay the vet bill to keep him alive after he suffered gastrointestinal irritation, tremors, difficulty breathing, or a coma from alcohol poisoning. If he doesn't suffer serious damage from the alcohol, he may still become a very sick dog.

Party foods can be a danger to dogs as well. Candies and gum that contain the sweetener xylitol can cause problems in dogs—a fairly sudden drop in blood sugar, resulting in depression and seizures—especially if large amounts are eaten. Chocolate in all forms—baking, semi-sweet, milk, and dark—can be potentially poisonous to dogs, depending on the amount eaten and the type of chocolate. Vomiting, diarrhea, seizures, hyperactivity, and increased thirst, urination and heart rate can be seen with the ingestion of as little as a quarter-ounce of baking chocolate by a 10-pound dog. Spicy and highly seasoned foods can cause stomach upset in most dogs, and pancreatitis in dogs who are prone to the problem.

Even ordinary foods can harm your dog if fed to him by unsuspecting guests. With "bloomin' onions" becoming popular party fare, it's important to know that onions can be extremely toxic to a dog's system. Depending on the amount ingested, they cause oxidative damage to the hemoglobins and result in an acute anemia. Either fresh or cooked onions can be toxic. If enough is ingested, it can even result in the need for a blood transfusion. Hemoglobin can be passed in the urine, so if your dog is not kept

Care and attention will keeep your best friend healthy for years to come.

well hydrated, his kidneys can be damaged as well. If you realize your dog has ingested onions, contact your veterinarian immediately and request emergency care.

Not only will your dog possibly be at risk of danger from foods or drink your guests might share with him, but it's likely that he could suffer a great deal of stress if he hasn't been properly socialized around large groups of noisy people. A careless guest may leave a door open long enough for your dog to escape without you knowing he's even missing in all the hubbub of the party.

It is best, if your party will be attended by a lot of non–dog people, that your dog is kept away from the festivities for his own good. Give him an acceptable treat and perhaps allow him to be part of the party only on a very limited, supervised basis.

Electric Shocks

Most people who are very careful about their use of extension cords during the rest of the year can get lax on safety issues in the holiday rush. If you must run cords to holiday lighting, run them through a length of PVC piping so that they're not accessible to your pets. Not only can your Basset suffer electric shocks from holiday lights, but he can become entangled in strings of lights, which can cause burns and cuts.

Choking Hazards

Even the best housekeepers can't keep track of all the extra clutter that is amassed during the holiday season. From staples and rubber bands, glue and ornament hangers, to small ornaments and packing peanuts—any small item is a potential choking hazard to a snoopy Basset.

Candles

The flame of a candle isn't the only hazard to your dog. Dripping wax can be extremely painful and can cause deep skin burns. Candles never should be left burning in a room with an unsupervised dog, not only for their personal safety, but because of the potential fire hazard to your entire home if a candle is knocked over.

Keep your Basset safe during holiday parties.

Plants

Most holiday-specific plants can be toxic to animals. Holly, mistletoe, ivy, and poinsettia can cause problems ranging from a mild stomach upset to an extreme toxic reaction. The first symptoms include nausea, vomiting, diarrhea, and excessive drooling. If your dog exhibits these symptoms you should seek medical attention immediately, because these can be a precursor of a coma, central nervous system, cardiac problems, and even death.

You should make sure that you know how to contact your vet during what may be a very erratic holiday schedule for her. If your regular vet's office will be closed, be certain you have information for a backup vet, as well as an emergency vet for after-hours.

THE AGING BASSET

There is no friend like an old friend. And no one could be dearer than an older dog who has been beside you through good times and bad. Like an old married couple, you are aware of each other's likes and dislikes, and he instinctively seems to know when you need a sloppy dog kiss after a tough day at work. You have learned

Be sure to have as few potential choking hazzards as possible in your Basset's environment.

191

to depend on each other for comfort, laughs, and companionship when the rest of the world seems to have turned its back. As much as you need your pet, he needs you—now more than ever before. Taking care of his special needs to ensure a long, healthy life proves your love for him will endure well into his golden years and beyond.

In general, senior dogs can't handle stress as well as younger dogs can. Sudden changes in routine, diet, or even the environment can play havoc with your older pet's health. A dog's body changes as it grows older, just as our human bodies do, and health problems become more commonplace, even expected.

I'm sure you may have always heard that 1 year of a dog's life equals 7 years of a human's life. Actually, however, by the time a dog is 1 year old, he has surpassed a 7-year-old child's development. Once a dog reaches adulthood, the aging over 1 year equals the aging that takes place in a human over 5 years.

It is difficult to determine an exact ratio for the aging process, because different breeds age at different rates. Larger dogs do not have as long a life expectancy as the smaller toy breeds. While a Great Dane may be considered elderly at age 6, a Basset Hound will

An aging but previously healthy Basset may begin to develop problems with his sight, hearing, and digestion, among others.

have just entered middle age at that time, and a Chihuahua will not be considered a senior citizen until he is well into his mid-teens.

The first step to caring for your older dog is to realize and accept that he is growing old. This isn't always easy to do. Some symptoms of aging appear gradually and are difficult to notice. You may not notice that your friend is graying around the muzzle until you look at a photograph of his earlier years and realize he now looks far different. If you notice (and accept) the changes that will occur as your pet ages, and allow them to be signals specifying the need for special care, you can ensure many additional quality years of love and affection from your aging but healthy pet.

Bowels

Your pet's bowel habits will change considerably as he ages. Constipation may be brought on by a loss of muscle tone in the bowel area, by insufficient water consumption, or, in older male dogs, by an enlargement of the prostate. Adding bran, cereal, or fresh vegetables to your dog's diet may provide the laxative effect necessary to get things moving again.

Deafness

One of the first signs of aging is when a dog who has always been responsive to your calls suddenly seems to be ignoring you. Usually, the sense of direction is the first portion of hearing to go. Try whistling to your pet and see if he turns in your direction. Purchasing a strong whistle to blow when you want your Basset's attention is often the trick to retaining good communication, because most dogs can hear high-pitched sounds long after other sounds disappear.

Dental Issues

It's extremely important to continue good dental habits with the older dog. Gum disease and tooth decay can cause heart problems resulting from the chronic release of bacteria into the circulatory system. By keeping your pet in good dental health, you will not only be making him easier to live with by avoiding foul breath, but you will be lengthening his life expectancy.

In addition to regular brushing, providing your dog with dental chews may help keep his teeth in good condition. Nylabone makes some good chews that are suited to a Basset's size and chewing power.

Older dogs may require a different exercise regimen to keep their hearts healthy.

Eye Anomalies

Older dogs may start to bump into things or appear generally disoriented. You may see a blue-gray tint to the eye. A canine ophthalmologist can tell you whether the diminished vision is actually due to increasing age or whether there is an underlying, possibly treatable condition.

Heart

The early detection of heart disease can prevent unnecessary pain and premature death. The earliest signal of heart failure is a low, deep, moist cough unaccompanied by mucous or signs of a cold. Treatment might include medication, as well as a change of diet and exercise. It's important that your vet give your senior pet a complete checkup to rule out medically treatable heart problems.

Incontinence

Your veterinarian can usually treat urinary incontinence in an older spayed female by prescribing medication. As dogs of both coxes become older and the sphincter muscle that keeps urine from escaping, loses muscle tissue, even the most well housetrained dog may have accidents. The older dog usually doesn't realize he is leaking, and should never be punished for accidents that he likely couldn't control, and of which he may have been totally unaware.

Kidneys

You may notice that your pet makes more trips to his water bowl as he gets older. An older dog may drink up to two or three times more water than a younger dog. Because his kidneys do not function as well as they age, he needs extra water to maintain their efficiency. You should always mention the excessive thirst to your vet.

Skin

The elasticity of the skin diminishes in all mammals as they age. Cuts and bruises that once would have healed in a matter of days may take a much longer time to disappear. Tiny, wartlike bumps may appear on your Basset's face and other parts of the body. He may begin shedding more frequently and more voluminously as he ages and becomes less active. None of these changes are cause for alarm, unless they seem to actually bother the dog in some way. Bumps and warts that are in danger of being continuously bruised or torn during grooming or daily activities should be removed.

Tumors and cysts seem to appear overnight on the older dog. Usually, these are benign cysts and fatty tumors. Since older dogs are more prone to malignancies than younger pets, you should always have any lump or bump checked by your veterinarian.

Weight

Dogs who always have been chow-hounds begging unrelentingly for additional food may suffer a loss of appetite as they pass more and more birthday landmarks. The older a dog gets, the more his sense of smell and taste weakens, so that he becomes less interested in food as time passes by. A decrease in weight may result from muscles becoming flabby as the older dog cuts back on both his food intake and his exercise. Your vet may suggest a change to a food formulated for senior dogs to help with the problems.

A dog—especially an older dog—who drinks a lot of water may be exihibiting signs of a kidney problem.

SAYING GOODBYE

How wonderful it would be if all our beloved pets that were ready to go did so in their sleep, without showing signs of illness. Although this does occur at times, it doesn't always, and it will likely be up to you to decide when the time has come to say goodbye. There is no easy way to make this decision. It is human nature to want to hold on as long as possible, to keep telling yourself that "tomorrow he'll be better," until it becomes apparent that your best friend's tomorrows will be filled only with the pain and confusion of his today—and that it is within your power to ease the pain and take away the confusion. This is not a selfish decision—quite the contrary. Giving your pet a painless death, and being with him through his final moments will likely be one of the hardest things any pet owner will ever be asked to do. It is the last gift you can give your old friend, and the most important. Discuss euthanasia with your veterinarian, as soon as your pet begins to give you signals that it may soon be time to go. Some vets who usually don't make regular house calls will make an exception for euthanasia. Most will allow or even request that the owner stay in the room with his pet until the shot has been administered and the final breaths have been taken. Don't worry about discomfort for your dog during those last moments of life. Euthanasia is simply the intravenous injection of an overdose of an anesthetic drug. Quite simply, your pet will blissfully fall into one last deep sleep. His last thoughts will be of you, and that you loved him enough to let him go.

ASSOCIATIONS AND ORGANIZATIONS

BREED CLUBS

American Kennel Club (AKC)
5580 Centerview Drive
Raleigh, NC 27606
Telephone: (919) 233-9767
Fax: (919) 233-3627
E-mail: info@akc.org
www.akc.org

Basset Hound Club (UK)
Secretary: Mrs. Joan Scott-
Goldstone
E-mail:
info@bassethoundclub.co.uk
www.bassethoundclub.co.uk

**Basset Hound Club of America
(BHCA)**
Secretary: Gwen McCullagh
E-mail: GwenM10100@aol.com
www.basset-bhca.org

Canadian Kennel Club (CKC)
89 Skyway Avenue, Suite 100
Etobicoke, Ontario M9W 6R4
Telephone: (416) 675-5511
Fax: (416) 675-6506
E-mail: information@ckc.ca
www.ckc.ca

**Federation Cynologique
Internationale (FCI)**
Secretariat General de la FCI
Place Albert 1er, 13
B – 6530 Thuin
Belqique
www.fci.be

The Kennel Club
1 Clarges Street
London
W1J 8AB
Telephone: 0870 606 6750
Fax: 0207 518 1058
www.the-kennel-club.org.uk

United Kennel Club (UKC)
100 E. Kilgore Road
Kalamazoo, MI 49002-5584
Telephone: (269) 343-9020
Fax: (269) 343-7037
E-mail: pbickell@ukcdogs.com
www.ukcdogs.com

RESCUE ORGANIZATIONS AND ANIMAL WELFARE GROUPS

**American Humane Association
(AHA)**
63 Inverness Drive East
Englewood, CO 80112
Telephone: (303) 792-9900
Fax: 792-5333
www.americanhumane.org

**American Society for the
Prevention of Cruelty to
Animals (ASPCA)**
424 E. 92nd Street
New York, NY 10128-6804
Telephone: (212) 876-7700
www.aspca.org

**Royal Society for the Prevention
of Cruelty to Animals (RSPCA)**
Telephone: 0870 3335 999
Fax: 0870 7530 284
www.rspca.org.uk

**The Humane Society of the
United States (HSUS)**
2100 L Street, NW
Washington DC 20037
Telephone: (202) 452-1100
www.hsus.org

SPORTS

Canine Freestyle Federation, Inc.
Secretary: Brandy Clymire
E-Mail: secretary@canine-
freestyle.org
www.canine-freestyle.org

International Agility Link (IAL)
Global Administrator: Steve
Drinkwater
E-mail: yunde@powerup.au
www.agilityclick.com/~ial

**North American Dog Agility
Council**
11522 South Hwy 3
Cataldo, ID 83810
www.nadac.com

**North American Flyball
Association (NAFA)**
1400 West Devon Avenue #512
Chicago, IL 60660
Telephone: (800) 318-6312
Fax: (800) 318-6318
www.flyball.org

**United States Dog Agility
Association**
P.O. Box 850955
Richardson, TX 75085-0955
Telephone: (972) 487-2200
www.usdaa.com

**World Canine Freestyle
Organization**
P.O. Box 350122
Brooklyn, NY 11235-2525
Telephone: (718) 332-8336
www.worldcaninefreestyle.org

VETERINARY RESOURCES

**Academy of Veterinary
Homeopathy (AVH)**
P.O. Box 9280
Wilmington, DE 19809
Telephone: (866) 652-1590
Fax: (866) 652-1590
E-mail: office@TheAVH.org
www.theavh.org

**American Academy of
Veterinary Acupuncture (AAVA)**
100 Roscommon Drive, Suite 320
Middletown, CT 06457
Telephone: (860) 635-6300
Fax: (860) 635-6400
E-mail: office@aava.org
www.aava.org

**American Animal Hospital
Association (AAHA)**
P.O. Box 150899
Denver, CO 80215-0899
Telephone: (303) 986-2800
Fax: (303) 986-1700
E-mail: info@aahanet.org
www.aahanet.org/index.cfm

**American College of Veterinary
Internal Medicine (ACVIM)**
1997 Wadsworth Blvd., Suite A
Lakewood, CO 80214-5293
Telephone: (800) 245-9081
Fax: (303) 231-0880
Email: ACVIM@ACVIM.org
www.acvim.org

**American College of Veterinary
Ophthalmologists (ACVO)**
P.O. Box 1311
Meridian, Idaho 83860
Telephone: (208) 466-7624
Fax: (208) 466-7693
E-mail: office@acvo.com
www.acvo.com

American Heartworm Society
PO Box 667
Batavia, IL 60510

E-mail:
heartwormsociety@earthlink.net
www.heartwormsociety.org

**American Holistic Veterinary
Medical Association (AHVMA)**
2218 Old Emmorton Road
Bel Air, MD 21015
Telephone: (410) 569-0795
Fax: (410) 569-2346
E-mail: office@ahvma.org
www.ahvma.org

**American Veterinary Medical
Association (AVMA)**
1931 North Meacham Road –
Suite 100
Schaumburg, IL 60173
Telephone: (847) 925-8070
Fax: (847) 925-1329
E-mail: avmainfo@avma.org
www.avma.org

**ASPCA Animal Poison Control
Center**
1717 South Philo Road, Suite 36
Urbana, IL 61802
Telephone: (888) 426-4435
www.aspca.org

**British Veterinary Association
(BVA)**
7 Mansfield Street
London
W1G 9NQ
Telephone: 020 7636 6541
Fax: 020 7436 2970
E-mail: bvahq@bva.co.uk
www.bva.co.uk

VMDB/CERF
1248 Lynn Hall
625 Harrison St.
Purdue University
West Lafayette, IN 47907-2026
Telephone: (765) 494-8179
E-mail: CERF@vmbd.org
www.vmdb.org

**Orthopedic Foundation for
Animals (OFA)**
2300 NE Nifong Blvd
Columbus, Missouri 65201-3856
Telephone: (573) 442-0418
Fax: (573) 875-5073
Email: ofa@offa.org
www.offa.org

MISCELLANEOUS
**Association of Pet Dog Trainers
(APDT)**
150 Executive Center Drive Box
35
Greenville, SC 29615

Telephone: (800) PET-DOGS
Fax: (864) 331-0767
E-mail: information@apdt.com
www.apdt.com

Delta Society
875 124th Ave NE, Suite 101
Bellevue, WA 98005
Telephone: (425) 226-7357
Fax: (425) 235-1076
E-mail: info@deltasociety.org
www.deltasociety.org

**National Association of
Professional Pet Sitters**
15000 Commerce Parkway, Suite
C
Mt. Laurel, NJ 08054
Telephone: (800) 296-PETS
Fax: (856) 439-0525
E-mail: napps@ahint.com
www.petsitters.org

Pet Sitters International
201 East King Street
King, NC 27021-9161
Telephone: (336) 983-9222
Fax: (336) 983-5266
E-mail: info@petsit.com
www.petsit.com

**Therapy Dogs International
(TDI)**
88 Bartley Road
Flanders, NJ 07836
Telephone: (973) 252-9800
Fax: (973) 252-7171
E-mail: tdi@gti.net
www.tdi-dog.org

MAGAZINES
AKC Family Dog
American Kennel Club
260 Madison Avenue
New York, NY 10016
Telephone: (800) 490-5675
E-mail: familydog@akc.org
www.akc.org/pubs/familydog

AKC Gazette
American Kennel Club
260 Madison Avenue
New York, NY 10016
Telephone: (800) 533-7323
E-mail: gazette@akc.org
www.akc.org/pubs/gazette

The Bugler
PO Box 698
McMinnville. TN 37110
E-mail: buglr@infoave.net

Dog & Kennel
Pet Publishing, Inc.

7-L Dundas Circle
Greensboro, NC 27407
Telephone: (336) 292-4272
Fax: (336) 292-4272
E-mail: info@petpublishing.com
www.dogandkennel.com

Dog Fancy
Subscription Department
P.O. Box 53264
Boulder, CO 80322-3264
Telephone: (800) 365-4421
E-mail: barkback@dogfancy.com
www.dogfancy.com

Dogs Monthly
Ascot House
High Street, Ascot,
Berkshire SL5 7JG
United Kingdom
Telephone: 0870 730 8433
Fax: 0870 730 8431
E-mail: admin@rtc-
associates.freeserve.co.uk
www.corsini.co.uk/dogsmonthly

WEBSITES
Agility Bassets
www.agilitybassets.com
Photos and information for
Basset owners interested in
agility.

Adopt a Dog
www.flex.net/~lonestar/basset.h
tm
Good link for Basset rescue
groups as well as a nice general
description of the Basset.

Boswell's Life of Boswell
www.basset.net/bostop.html
Browse the pages of an antique
book featuring Boswell the Basset
Hound.

Dogfriendly.com
www.dogfriendly.com
Dog travel guide for the US and
Canada.

Dogpark.com
www.dogpark.com
Listing of dog parks across the
country, along with tips for being
a good dog-parker and lots of
other great doggy links.

Petswelcome.com
www.petswelcome.com
Large pet/travel resource site
with hotels, ski resorts,
campgrounds, and beaches that
are pet-friendly.

Note: **Boldfaced** numbers indicate
   illustrations.

A

Abbey of St. Hubert, 5
Acceptable vs. Unacceptable
   behaviors, 99–100
Accidents in housetraining, 104,
   105–108
Acupuncture, 175
Addison's disease, 75
Adenovirus, 157
Adult dogs
   adoption of, 32–35
   feeding, 62, 70–72, **70**
   problem behaviors in, 44
   rescue organizations and, 43–44
Age equivalents, man vs. Dog, 180,
   192
Aggression, 126–127
Agility competition, 132–134, **133**
Air travel, 55
Alexandra, Queen of England, 8–9
Allen, Steve, 14–15
Allergies, 158–159, 167
   Nambrudipad's Allergy
      Elimination Technique
      (NAET), 178
Aloe vera lotion, 171
America and the Basset Hound,
   9–11
American Boarding Kennel
   Association (ABKA), 56
American Kennel Club (AKC), 9,
   11, 12
   breed standard of, 18
   Canine Good Citizen (CGC)
      program, 134–137
   pedigrees and, 37
   registering your dog with, 34, 37
Anal sac care, 86–87
Animal behaviorists, 119–120
Annual health checkups, 154–156
Anthony of St. Hubert, 11
Aromatherapy, 175
Arthritis, 74
Artificial coloring/flavoring in
   foods, 62
Association of American Feed
   Control Officials (AAFCO), 63
Attention requirements, 23–24
Ayurvedic medicine, 175

B

Back problems, 170–171
Bad breath, 91
Barking, 24, 121, 123

Basset Hound Club, 8
Basset Hound Club of America
   (BHCA), 10, 11
Bathing your Basset Hound, 83–86
Begging at table, 78–79
Beginner's Guide to Dog Shows, A,
   139
Biting, 123–124
Blaze, Elzear, 5
Bloat (gastric torsion), 158, 159–161
Blood diseases, 162, 164–165
Bloodhound, 9, 11
Blue Basset Hound, 23
Blue-eyed Basset Hound, 23
Boarding kennels, 56–57
Body language of dogs, 122
Body shape and size, 19
Bonding with your Basset Hound,
   93
Bones and joints
   arthritis and, 74
   cruciate ligament tears and, 74
   elbow dysplasia and, 39
   hip dysplasia and, 39, 74
   Institute for Genetic Disease
      Control in Animals (GDC), 39
   intervertebral disk disease as,
      170–171
   Lyme disease and, 173
   meniscal injury as, 74
   Ontario Veterinary College
      (OVC) testing and, 39
   Orthopedic Foundation for
      Animals (OFA) and, 39
   panosteitis (wandering lame-
      ness, puppy limp) as, 171
   PennHip studies and, 39
   radiographs and x-rays of, 39
Bones and raw foods (BARF) diet,
   64–67
Bones in diet, 64–67
Books about the Basset Hound, 13
Bowel problems, 193
Bowls for food and water, 50
Brandt, Walter and Marge, 10
Breed clubs, 11
Breed standard, 17, 18, 140
Breeder screening, 39–43
Breeding of the Basset Hound, 6–9
Breeding your Basset Hound, 32,
   39
Brettenham, Mrs. Elis, 8
Brushing your Basset Hound,
   81–82, **82**, 83
Brushing your dog's teeth, **88**,
   89–90

Burns, 190
By-products in food, 60

C

Cancer, 166–167
Candles, safety, 190
Canine Eye Registration
   Foundation (CERF), 39, 167
Canine Good Citizen (CGC) pro-
   gram, 134–137, 145
Canine thrombopathia, 164
Canned dog food, 59
Car travel, 54–55
Carbohydrates in diet, 60
Carhart, Ewing, 11
Championship levels in conforma-
   tion, 139
Chewing, 90–92
Children and the Basset Hound,
   25–27, **26**, 31, 53
Chiropractic, 175–176
Choking, Heimlich maneuver and,
   172, 190
City life and the Basset Hound, 23
Cleaning up messes, 104–108
Cleo (*The People's Choice* TV show),
   12–13
Clubs and organizations, 11
Coach, TV show, 14
Coat and skin, 20–21, 74
   allergies and, 158–159, 167
   aloe vera as soothing lotion for,
      171
   grooming and, 83
   self-mutilation/licking, 129
   senior dogs and, 195
Collars, 48–49, 111–113
Colors, 20–21, 23
Columbo TV show, 13
Come command, 116, 118
Communicating with your Basset
   Hound, 122
Companionship and your Basset
   Hound, 32
Complementary and alternative
   vet medicine (CAVM) for,
   174–179
Conditioning for a show, 143
Conformation shows, 140–145
   age requirements for, 140–141
   breed standard and, 140
   championship levels in, 139
   conditioning for, 143
   dressing for, 144
   professional handlers for, 143,
      145
   show vs. pet quality dogs for,

The Basset Hound

35–38
stacking for, **138, 141**
training for, 141–143
winning attitude in, 137
Coprophagia (feces eating), 124–125
Corn in diet, 60
Coronavirus, 157
Cost of ownership, 32
Country life and the Basset Hound, 23
Crates and crate training, 48, 101
time limits to, 102
Cruciate ligament tears, 74
Crufts Dog Show, 132
Cushing's disease, 75

D
Day care for dogs, 56
Deafness, 193
Dental care, 74, **88**, 89–92
bad breath and, 91
brushing your dog's teeth in, **88**, 89–90
chewing and chew toys for, 90–92
senior dogs and, 193
Diabetes, 75
Digging, 125–126
Distemper, 157
Dog years, age equivalents, man vs. dog, 180, 192
Dog, on *Columbo*, 13
Doggie day care, 56
Doggie Stew recipe, 68
Dohr, Jim and Pat, 11
Down command, 117
Dressing for a dog show, 144
Drooling, 25
Dry food (kibble), 59
Drying your wet dog, 85–86
Dukes of Hazzard, 13
Dunbar, Ian, 149

E
Ears, 17–18
cleaning and care of, 87–88, **87**
deafness and, 193
infections in, 167
Ectropion and entropion, 167
Elbow dysplasia, 39
Electrical shock, 189–190
Emergency, TV show, 13
End-of-life issues, 196–197
Energy medicine, 176
England and the Basset Hound, 6–8
Environmental medicine, 176
Ethoxyquin as preservative, 62

Exercise needs, 23
Eyes, 18, 74
Canine Eye Registration Foundation (CERF) and, 39, 167
cleaning and care of, 88–89
ectropion and entropion in, 167
glaucoma and, 39, 167–168
gonioscopy for, 39
senior dogs and, 193–194

F
Famous Basset Hounds, 12–15
Fear of loud noises, 127–128
Fédération Cynologique Internationale, 12
Feeding, 49, 59–79
adult dogs, 62, 70–72, **70**
allergies and, 158–159, 167, 178
artificial coloring/flavoring in, 62
Association of American Feed Control Officials (AAFCO) standards and, 63
bloat (gastric torsion) and, 158, 159–161
bones and raw foods (BARF) diet in, 64–67
bones and, 64–67
bowls for, 50
by-products in, 60
canned food in, 59
choosing a commercial food for, 62–64
coprophagia (feces eating) and, 124–125
corn and carbohydrates in, 60
Doggie Stew recipe for, 68
dry food (kibble) in, 59
ethoxyquin as preservative in, 62
health and, 72, 73
Holy Mackerel Cakes recipe for, 69
homecooked diets in, 67–70
label contents of dog food in, 59–62
obesity and, 62–63, 74–78, 171, 195
preservatives in, 61, 62
protein in, 60
puppies, 62, 70–72, **70**
Pupsicles recipe for, 74
schedule for, 70–72, **70**
semi-moist food in, 59
senior dogs, 62, 70–73, **70**
storage of foods for, 49

table manners and, 78–79
Tasty Meatballs recipe for, 69
unsafe foods and, 188–189
Feet, 20
Fencing, 47
Field trials, 10, 11, 139
Find the Treat game, 148
Fino de Paris, 8
First-aid, 179–181
Flash, on *Dukes of Hazzard*, 13
Flea control, 84, 173–174
Follow the Leader game, 149
France and the Basset Hound, 5
"Free to good home" dogs, 32
French Revolution, 5

G
Galway, Lord, 6, 8
Games to play with your Basset Hound, 148–149
Garry Moore Show, italic, 13–14
Gastric torsion. *See* bloat
Genetic testing, 39
Giardia, 171–172
Gift puppies, 49
Glaucoma, 39, 167–168
Gonioscopy, 39
Gordon, Dick, 13
Grooming, 25, 81–93
anal sac care in, 86–87
bathing in, 83–86
bonding time during, 93
brushing in, 81–82, **82**, 83
dental care in, **88**, 89–92
drying in, 85–86
ear care in, 87–88, **87**
eye care in, 88–89
flea control and, 84
importance of, 81
nail care in, 92–93, **92**
shampoos and conditioners in, 84–85
shedding and, 82–83
skin health and, 83
supplies for, 50
table for, **85**
Grooming table, **85**
Guard dog, 32

H
Hamlin's Dolly, 11
Harnesses, 114–115
Hazards around the house, 46–47
Head, 17–18
Health issues, 151–197
acupuncture in, **175**
Addison's disease as, 75

adenovirus as, 157
age equivalents and, man vs. dog, 180, 192
allergies as, 158–159, 167, 178
anal sac care and, 86–87
annual health checks and, 154–156
aromatherapy in, 175
arthritis as, 74
Ayurvedic medicine in, 175
back problems as, 170–171
bad breath, 91
bloat (gastric torsion) as, 158, 159–161
blood diseases as, 162, 164–165
bowel problems as, 193
burns as, 190
cancer as, 166–167
Canine Eye Registration Foundation (CERF) and, 39, 167
canine thrombopathia as, 164
chiropractice in, 175–176
choking as, 190
complementary and alternative vet medicine (CAVM) for, 174–179
coprophagia (feces eating) as, 124–125
coronavirus as, 157
cost of, 32
cruciate ligament tears as, 74
deafness as, 193
dental care in, **88**, 89–92, 193
diabetes as, 75
distemper as, 157
ears and, 87–88, **87**, 167
ectropion and entropion as, 167
elbow dysplasia as, 39
electrical shock and, 189–190
end-of-life issues and, 196–197
energy medicine in, 176
environmental medicine in, 176
eyes and, 88–89, 167, 193–194
feeding and, 72, 73
first-aid and, 179–181
flea control and, 84, 173–174
foods to avoid and, 188–189
genetic testing and, 39
Giardia as, 171–172
glaucoma as, 39, 167–168
gonioscopy and, 39
hazards around the house and, 46–47
health tips and, 166

heart problems as, 194
heartworm as, 173
Heimlich maneuver and, 172
herbal medicine in, 176
hip dysplasia as, 39, 74
holistic medicine and, 170, 176
homeopathy in, 177
hookworm as, 172
housetraining accidents and, 108
housetraining and, 194–195
hyperadrenocorticism (Cushing's disease) as, 75
hypothyroidism as, 39, 75, 168–170
incontinence as, 194–195
Institute for Genetic Disease Control in Animals (GDC) and, 39
intervertebral disk disease as, 170–171
kidney problems as, 195
kinesiology in, 177
leptospirosis as, 157
liquid medication and, 185
Lyme disease as, 173
massage therapy in, 178
meniscal injury as, 74
Nambrudipad's Allergy Elimination Technique (NAET) in, 178
obesity as, 62–63, 74–78, 171, 195
Ontario Veterinary College (OVC) testing and, 39
Orthopedic Foundation for Animals (OFA) and, 39
panosteitis (wandering lameness, puppy limp) as, 171
parainfluenza as, 158
parvovirus as, 157
patellar luxation as, 39
PennHip and, 39
pilling your dog for, 178
poisoning, poison plants and, 181–184, 191
puppy's first vet visit and, 151
rabies as, 158
radiographs and x-rays in, 39
reflexology in, 178
roundworm as, 172
self-mutilation/licking as, 129
senior dogs and, 191–197
shedding and, 82–83
shiatsu in, 178
skin health and, 83, 195
spaying and neutering in, 153,

154
sports safety and, 143
tapeworm as, 173
Tellington Touch in, 178
temperament evaluation and, 39
therapeutic touch in, 178–179
thrombopathy (blood platelet disorder) as, 39
thyroid problems as, 168–170
tick control and, 173–174
umbilical hernias as, 153
vaccinations in, 157–158
veterinarian selection for, 151–152
vital signs and, normal values for, 179–180
von Willebrand's disease (vWD) as, 39, 162, 164
when to call the vet in, 163
whipworm as, 172–173
worms and worming in, 171–173
Health tips, 166
Heart problems, 194
Heartworm, 173
Heel command, 118–119
Height and weight, 21
Heimlich maneuver, 172
Henry, on *Emergency* TV show, 13
Herbal medicine, 176
Hide and Go Seek game, 149
Hillcrest Peggy, 10
Hip dysplasia, 39, 74
History of the Basset Hound, 5–15
Holidays and your Basset Hound, 49, 188–190
Holistic medicine, 170, 174–179
Holy Mackerel Cakes recipe for, 69
Homecooked diets, 67–70
Homeopathy, 177
Hookworm, 172
Hotels, motels and your Basset Hound, 55–56
Housetraining, 101, 104–108
accidents in, 104, 105–108
health issues and accidents in, 108, 194–195
incontinence and, 194–195
Hunting, 5, 11, 139
tracking competition and, 147–148
Hush Puppies and the Basset Hound, 15
Hyperadrenocorticism (Cushing's disease), 75
Hypothyroidism, 39, 75, 168–170

I

ID tags, 50, 187
Incontinence, 194–195
Institute for Genetic Disease
   Control in Animals (GDC), 39
Intelligence, 9

J

Jason and the Hush Puppies Co., 15
Juley von Skauton, Ch., 132
Jumping up, 128–129, **128**

K

Kazoo's Moses the Great, 11
Kennel Club, 11, 12
   breed standard of, 18
   registering your dog with, 34, 37
Kidney problems, 195
Kinesiology, 177
Kini, 8
Krehl, George, 6, 7, 8

L

Label contents of dog foods, 59–62
Lady Daisy, 8
Lady Dollie, 8
Lane kennels, 6, 8
Le Chasseur, 5
Le Couteulx kennels, 6, 8
Le Venerie de Jacques du Fouillou, 5
Leash training, 109–116
Leashes, 48–49, 115–116
Legs, 19–20
Leptospirosis, 157
Liquid medication, administering,
   185
Lost dogs, 184–188
Ludwig von B, 11
Lulu's Red, 10
Lyme disease, 173

M

Massage therapy, 178
McWilliams' Dixie Belle, 11
McWilliams, Ken, 11
Meniscal injury, 74
Microchipping, 50
Millais, Everett, 6–9
Model, 6, 8
Morgan, on the *Garry Moore Show*,
   13–14
Movement, 21
Movies and the Basset Hound,
   12–15, 32
My Dog Can Do That game, 149

N

Nail care, 92–93, **92**

Nambrudipad's Allergy
   Elimination Technique (NAET),
   178
National Association of
   Professional Pet Sitters, 57
No More Bad Breath Biscuit recipe,
   91
Nose, 17
Nylabone, 48, 51, 92, 193

O

Obedience classes, 134
Obedience competition, 137–138
Obesity, 62–63, 74–78, 171, 195
Onslow, Lord, 6, 7, 8
Ontario Veterinary College (OVC)
   testing, 39
Origins of the breed, 5
Orthopedic Foundation for
   Animals (OFA), 39
Other pets and the Basset Hound,
   24, 52, 95–98
Outdoor play, 25

P

Panosteitis (wandering lameness,
   puppy limp), 171
Parainfluenza, 158
Parasites. *See* flea control; tick con-
   trol; worms and worming
Parvovirus, 157
Patellar luxation, 39
PATSY winners, 12–13
Pedigrees, 37
PennHip, 39
People's Choice, The, 12–13
Pet sitters, 57
Pet vs. Show quality dogs, 35–38
Pettit, Tom, 11
Pickup truck travel, 53
Pilling your dog, 178
Plants, poisonous, 181–184, 191
Poison Control Center Hotline
   Number, 183
Poisoning, poison plants, 181–184,
   191
Popularity of the Basset Hound, 9,
   32
Positive training methods, 101
Preservatives in food, 61, 62
Presley, Elvis, 14–15
Problem behaviors, 44, 98, 119–129
   acceptable vs. unacceptable
     behaviors and, 99–100
   aggression, dog-on-dog, 126–127
   barking as, 24, 121, 123

   begging, table manners and,
     78–79
   behavior consultants for, 119–120
   biting as, 123–124
   coprophagia (feces eating) as,
     124–125
   digging as, 125–126
   fear of loud noises as, 127–128
   jumping up as, 128–129, **128**
   self-mutilation/licking as, 129
Professional handlers, for showing,
   143
Professional trainers, 110
Pros and cons of Basset Hound
   ownership, 28
Proteins in food, 60
Puppies
   adult dog adoption vs., 32–35
   American Temperament Test
     Society Inc. and, 39
   biting in, 123–124
   breeder screening for, 39–43
   bringing puppy home, 45
   children and, 53
   conformation shows and,
     140–141
   feeding, 62, 70–72, **70**
   first day home, 51
   genetic testing in, 39
   gifts/as gifts, 49
   introducing other pets to, 52,
     95–98
   introducing people to, 52, 95–98
   kindergarten for, 98
   panosteitis (wandering lame-
     ness, puppy limp) as, 171
   pedigrees for, 37
   Puppy Aptitude Test for, 39
   puppy proofing the home for,
     46–47
   registration of, 34, 37
   show vs. pet quality, 35–38
   socialization in, 95–98
   sources for, 38–39
   spaying and neutering in, 153,
     154
   temperament evaluation in, 39
   umbilical hernias in, 153
   vaccinations in, 157–158
   veterinarian care for, 151
   worms and worming in, 152,
     171–173
Puppy kindergarten, 98
Puppy proofing the home, 46–47
Pupsicles recipe, 74

Purina Pet Institute feeding studies, 72

Q

Quincy, on *Coach*, 14
Quiz, are you right for the Basset Hound?, 27–29

R

Rabies, 158
Radiographs and x–rays, 39
Reflexology, 178
Registering your Basset Hound, 34, 37
Rescue organizations, 43–44
Resources, 201–202
Robert, M., 5
Roundworm, 172
Royalty and the Basset Hound, 8–9
Rules for your Basset Hound, 98–100, 123
Ryan, Terry, 149

S

Sandberg, Stephen and Anna, 11
Seitz, Emil and Effie, 10
Self-mutilation/licking, 129
Semi-moist food, 59
Senior dogs, 191–197
    age equivalents, man vs. dog, 192
    bowel problems and, 193
    deafness and, 193
    dental health and, 193
    end-of-life issues and, 196–197
    eyes and, 193–194
    feeding, 62, 70–73, **70**
    health care and health issues of, 191–197
    heart problems and, 194
    incontinence and, 194–195
    kidney problems and, 195
    skin problems and, 195
    weight issues and, 195
Service dogs, 145–147, **146**
Shakespeare and the Basset Hound, 8
Shampoos and conditioners, 84–85
Shedding, 82–83, 82
Sherlock and Steve Allen, 14–15
Shiatsu, 178
Show vs. pet quality dogs, 35–38
Showing your Basset Hound. *See* conformation shows
Sit command, 116–117
Skin. *See* coat and skin
Socialization, 95–98

Spaying and neutering, 153, 154
Sports safety, 143
Stacking for a show, **138**, **141**
Stay command, 117–118
Storage of foods, 49
Sullivan, Ed, 14

T

Table manners, 78–79
Tail, 20
Tapeworm, 173
Tasty Meatballs recipe for, 69
Teeth, 18, 74. *See also* dental care
Television and the Basset Hound, 12–15, 32
Tellington Touch, 178
Temperament, 21-22, 28
    American Temperament Test Society Inc. (ATTS), 39
    Puppy Aptitude Test for, 39
Therapeutic touch, 178–179
Therapy dogs, 145–147, **146**
Thrombopathy (blood platelet disorder), 39, 164
Thyroid problems, 168–170
Tick control, 173–174
Toys, 51
    chewing and dental health using, 90–92
    hazards of, 47
Tracking competition, 147–148
Training, 24–25, 95–129
    acceptable vs. unacceptable behaviors and, 99–100
    body language of dogs and, 122
    Canine Good Citizen (CGC) program and, 134–137
    collars for, 111–113
    Come command in, 116, 118
    conformation showing and, 141–143
    cost of, 32
    crates and, 101
    Down command in, 117
    harnesses for, 114–115
    Heel command in, 118–119
    housetraining and, 101, 104–108
    leash training and, 109–116
    leashes for, 115–116
    obedience classes and, 134
    obedience competition and, 137–138
    positive methods in, 101
    problem behaviors and. *See* problem behaviors
    professional trainers for, 110

    puppy kindergarten and, 98
    rule setting for, 98–100, 123
    Sit command in, 116–117
    socialization in, 95–98
    Stay command in, 117–118
    table manners and, 78–79
    your leadership role in, 100
Traveling with your Basset Hound, 53–56
Trucks and travel, 53

U

Umbilical hernias, 153

V

Vaccinations, 157–158
Van's Fantasy, 11
Veterinarian selection, 151–152
Vital signs for your Basset Hound, 179–180
Von Willebrand's disease (vWD), 39, 162, 164

W

Walking with your Basset Hound, 109–116, 118–119
Wardle, Arthur, 9
Washbond, Mark, 11
Watchdogs, 32
Water sports and the Basset Hound, 21
Weight, 21. *See also* obesity
Westminster Kennel Club dog show, 9
When to call the vet, 163
Whipworm, 172–173
Why do you want a dog?, 31–32
Working dogs, 100
World Canine Organization, 12
Worms and worming, 152, 171–173

ACKNOWLEDGEMENTS
Thanks to Rick Clark for continuing to be the world's best
researcher....and friend. And to Peter Land and Bill Lee for always
"being there."

ABOUT THE AUTHOR
Bobbye ("Babs") Land shares her Alabama farm home with a myriad of pets including, in order
of size, a horse (Story), a cow (Elizabeth), a goat (Daisy), 4 dogs (Michael, Dixie, Rose and Halle),
a cat (Merlin Monroe), a conure (Chuckles) and 3 dwarf hamsters. She is active in English cocker
rescue as well as always being willing to offer a foster home to any animal in need. An avid
wildlife watcher, her home is a wildlife haven. Her work resume includes not only years as a
writer (with multiple books, magazine articles and columns) but also 25 years breeding and
exhibiting purebred dogs, 7 years as a veterinary assistant, and 7 years as the owner/manager of
a pet grooming shop.

PHOTO CREDITS
Photos on page 88, 97 courtesy of Paulette Braun
Photo on page 136 courtesy of Joy Brown (Shutterstock)
Photos on page 21, 148 courtesy of Robert Pearcy
Photos on page 64, 100, 108, 132 courtesy of Vince Serbin
Photos on page 69, 125 courtesy of Lara Stern
All other photos courtesy of Isabelle Francais and TFH archives

NATURAL with added VITAMINS
Nutri Dent ®
MD
Promotes Optimal Dental Health!

Visit nylabone.com
Join Club NYLA
for coupons &
product
information

360° Design
Cleaning Action!™

Dog's L♥ve'em!™

AVAILABLE IN MULTIPLE SIZES AND FLAVORS.

Nylabone®

Trusted For Over 40 Years

MADE IN THE USA

Our Mission with Nutri Dent® is to promote optimal dental health for dogs through a trusted, natural, delicious chew that provides effective cleaning action...GUARANTEE to make your dog go wild with anticipation and happiness!!!

Nylabone Products • P.O. Box 427, Neptune, NJ 07754-0427 • 1-800-631-2188 • Fax: 732-988-5466
www.nylabone.com • info@nylabone.com • For more information contact your sales representative or contact us at sales@tfh.com